Suanne Beverly

The Kitchenless™ Cookbook

InterMedia Publishing, Inc.

 Contents of this page continue on page 220.

Illustrations by Walter Gallup

Design, Additional Illustrations, and Layout by Joanne Slike

Library of Congress Catalog Card No.: 97-81194
ISBN 0-9662137-0-X

First Edition

Printed in the United States of America

10 9 8 7 6 5 4 3 2 1

InterMedia Publishing, Inc.
P.O. Box 291506
Davie, FL 33329-1506

Printed in the USA by
WIMMER
The Wimmer Companies
Memphis

For Cicely —
you always knew

Acknowledgments

This book could never have happened without the help of dozens of people. My test kitchen helpers were more fun than a college football weekend! Thanks to Melissa Nye, Fernando Yanez, Felipe Gaitan, David de la Rosa, Erin Pollock, Missy Mignano, Michael Duncun, Misty Simmons, Erin Amelung, Genie Amelung, Stephanie Sandler, Nichole Jeroy, Brian Connor, Frank Miraglia, Autumn Smith, Chad Ford, Steve Labadie, Rebecca Cappiello, Christine Travieso, Jennie Johnson, Andy Steinberg, Rich Potter, and the student editors Ross Spense, Ajay Patel, Brad Schoenfeldt, and Morgan Pierce. Carol Jeroy once again proved I can't have a party without her.

Pat Soule Coate was my constant helper and confidant and always thought there was a book in this head. Wow, she was right. Susan Wolbarst listened to all my whining for months, transcoastal . . . we've come a long way since BMHS. Thanks to Buddy Robertson, the first chef in my life, who spent a busman's holiday finding my mistakes and Bobby for letting me borrow him.

My family — Brad, Morgan, and Glenn — you have been the test kitchen for life. Thank you for putting up with me. I love you.

Jesse and Mindy, you are super. I promise I'll stop calling now.

Also, goodbye to my editor — I already changed my phone number!

Contents

Introduction

This is a special kind of a cookbook. It is intended for those of us who have to squeeze the necessity of eating, even of eating somewhat nutritiously and well, into impossible schedules or taxing surroundings. If you are a college student living in a dorm, a single or pair in a small apartment, a boater or RV camper, physically challenged, or one of the millions of us stressed by time and work who want to (or must) eat when the opportunity strikes, this is the book for you. It is an alternative to unhealthy fast food joints and pizza take-outs; uninspired school or corporate cafeterias; expensive, slow-moving restaurants; or highly processed frozen foods.

There are 124 recipes here, none of which requires more than a microwave or a blender, most of which will have you eating in less than 20 minutes. And all of the recipes are easy, nutritious, cheap, and magically need only a shoeboxful of staples.

This is a practical book for busy people, whether you're cramming for a report or exam, or squeezing in a meal before or between work, school, or chauffeuring the kids around town. The recipes are creative and compact — with the accent always on the quick and easy preparation of tasty, nutritious, satisfying meals. There are no fancy cooking terms, and you definitely need no skill or previous experience in the kitchen. A teaspoon is a teaspoon, a Tablespoon (I always use a capital "T") is a soup spoon, and a cup is an empty yogurt cup. That's about as technical as it gets. I created and tested each recipe, then had a panel of youthful, inexperienced cooks do the same. Only the raves got through this torture test.

By the way, I got the idea for this book when several young working adults complained to me about the problem of eating well with their hectic lives, followed by a complaint by my college-aged kid who said she and her friends needed help eating at school. Their schedules forced them to eat poorly — the wrong things at the wrong time — in my daughter's case despite being on the school meal plan. I'm a professional chef, a certified cooking teacher, and caterer. I was always greatly concerned about my kids' diet, starting with feeding them homemade baby food. So, to make myself — as well as them — feel better, I decided to put everything else aside and create a book for real people in the real world.

Stuff to Read

... so you don't hurt yourself
and kill the cat

Your microwave oven

Appliances are like cars. Most people don't really care how they operate as long as they get you where you want to go. If you are really interested in the workings of your machine, the manufacturer has included a handy book outlining its inner mysteries.

Do thoroughly read the instruction book that comes with your oven
Do keep your oven clean, but **don't** use abrasive cleaners
Do use only microwave-safe glass or plastic containers
Do use potholders to remove food from the oven — the containers get very **hot**
Don't use any metal containers or products in the oven
Don't overcrowd the oven — cook one dish at a time
Don't attempt to operate the oven with the door open
Don't try to repair a broken appliance; bring it to a qualified technician

Knives

Do buy the best you can afford — they will work better, make things easier for you, and last a lifetime
Do use a cutting board; it saves both the knife and your counter
Do keep your knives clean by washing carefully and separately
Don't store them in a drawer; it dulls the knife and you risk a cut if you grab the wrong end

Food Storage

Do keep all dry food in air-tight containers
Do keep cold food cold and hot food hot to avoid bacterial growth
Do pay careful attention to "use by" dates on food packages — "*If in doubt, throw it out*"
Don't store partially used cans in the original container, transfer to glass or plastic
Don't drink milk or orange juice out of the container (yes, I'm a MOM!)

ALWAYS WASH YOUR HANDS BEFORE AND AFTER PREPARING FOOD

COOKING STUFF—BUYING TIPS

Just so you understand that you don't have to rush out to the local discount store and spend a week's earnings on matched sets of plastic and glassware, here are some handy alternatives to the beautifully illustrated list found on the following pages.

A cup needs to hold 8 ounces of material — liquid or solid. Although those liquid measures with the little pour spouts are useful, they are unnecessary. A yogurt container holds 8 ounces and works just fine as a measure. You can "eyeball" a half a yogurt cup for a 1/2-cup measure. Also, a normal-sized coffee cup holds about the same. A coffee mug, however, is generally 10 to 12 ounces, so don't use those.

A teaspoon is a teaspoon, like you stir your coffee with. A Tablespoon can be a soup spoon. Also, you can stir and serve with any spoons you have available. Paper plates can be substituted for the glass pie plate.

You can pare fruits and vegetables with a knife, eliminating the need for a vegetable peeler. This technique *does* require some skill mastery, however. Any recipe that calls for grated anything can be accomplished by cutting or chopping the food into tiny pieces instead. So, if you can't find (or don't want) a grater, just chop the stuff up finely.

I'd like you to buy a vegetable brush, but an **unsoaped** scrubbing pad works well too. As for potholders, the dishtowels can double if you're really strapped for cash. Just make sure they're dry because water conducts heat.

A can opener, cutting board, knife, and strainer are musts, but don't forget flea markets, garage sales, and thrift shops as sources for all the gear. Also, Mom, Grandma, and Aunt Lily usually have spares. It's often productive to "shop at home" for the best bargains.

SHOPPING LIST OF STUFF YOU NEED

before you cook (but check out page 12)

(you can tear this page out — we even give you a spare copy!!)

Appliances

- ☐ 700-watt or better microwave oven, if you can — a smaller oven may just mean longer zapping times*
- ☐ Inexpensive blender
- ☐ Access to a refrigerator and sink

Gear *(see pages 17 & 18 for pictures and exciting explanations)*

- ☐ Manual can opener
- ☐ Spatula
- ☐ Plastic ladle
- ☐ Large plastic mixing spoon
- ☐ Cutting board
- ☐ Strainer
- ☐ Grater (4-sided "box" ***or*** flat — *see page 52*)
- ☐ 1-quart microwave-safe glass bowl
- ☐ 2-1/2-quart microsafe glass bowl
- ☐ ~~6 microsafe glass custard cups~~
- ☐ 1-quart microsafe glass measuring pitcher
- ☐ 1-cup glass measuring cup with spout
- ☐ Plastic measuring spoons
- ☐ 9-inch microsafe pie plate
- ☐ Vegetable brush
- ☐ Vegetable peeler
- ☐ Sharp paring knife
- ☐ Sharp chef's knife
- ☐ 2 potholders
- ☐ 2 dish towels
- ☐ Plastic wrap
- ☐ Paper towels

* All the recipes in this book have been tested with a 700-watt microwave oven with a carousel. This is a small, convenient appliance. If yours is larger, you should decrease cooking time; if smaller, increase time. If it's really bigger, wear a radiation suit.

STUFF

SPICES & CONDIMENTS*

Try to purchase all these spices and condiments first (if you're in college, do this while your parents are still in town and they can help pay for them). All these things fit into a space about the size of a shoe box, so they can easily be stored under the bed or in some other out-of-the-way place. None requires refrigeration except the mayonnaise after you open it. In our shopping list section (pages 31 to 38), all of the condiments listed below will appear with a "+", meaning you already have them — if you've bought everything on this list. Incidentally, you can make healthier substitutes (low-fat mayonnaise, low-sodium soy sauce, etc.) if you wish.

The amount shown here, in the smallest available container, should last a single person about one year.

The stuff

- ☑ Apple cider vinegar
- ☑ Black pepper
- ☐ Chicken bouillon (granulated *or* cubes)
- ☑ Chili powder
- ☑ Cinnamon
- ☑ Cooking spray
- ☐ Cornstarch
- ☐ Curry powder
- ☑ Dried dill
- ☑ Garlic powder
- ☑ Ginger
- ☐ Hot sauce (Tabasco, or whatever)
- ☑ Italian seasoning
- ☐ Ketchup
- ☐ Mayonnaise
- ☐ Mustard
- ☑ Paprika
- ☐ Salt
- ☑ Seasoned salt (any brand)
- ☐ Soy sauce
- ☐ Vanilla
- ☐ Vegetable bouillon (granulated *or* cubes)
- ☐ Worcestershire sauce

* *Can they tear out this page, too?—Editor*

Folks, meet my "editor." She wants to know if you can tear this page out, too. Maybe she's figured out how to tear the other side out and leave this side in the book. This proves *anybody* can get a job in America.—Author

SHOPPING LIST OF STUFF YOU NEED

before you cook (but check out page 12)

(you can tear this page out — we even give you a spare copy!!)

Appliances

- ☐ 700-watt or better microwave oven, if you can — a smaller oven may just mean longer zapping times*
- ☐ Inexpensive blender
- ☐ Access to a refrigerator and sink

Gear *(see pages 17 & 18 for pictures and exciting explanations)*

- ☐ Manual can opener
- ☐ Spatula
- ☐ Plastic ladle
- ☐ Large plastic mixing spoon
- ☐ Cutting board
- ☐ Strainer
- ☐ Grater (4-sided "box" ***or*** flat — *see page 52*)
- ☐ 1-quart microwave-safe glass bowl
- ☐ 2-1/2-quart microsafe glass bowl
- ☐ 6 microsafe glass custard cups
- ☐ 1-quart microsafe glass measuring pitcher
- ☐ 1-cup glass measuring cup with spout
- ☐ Plastic measuring spoons
- ☐ 9-inch microsafe pie plate
- ☐ Vegetable brush
- ☐ Vegetable peeler
- ☐ Sharp paring knife
- ☐ Sharp chef's knife
- ☐ 2 potholders
- ☐ 2 dish towels
- ☐ Plastic wrap
- ☐ Paper towels

* All the recipes in this book have been tested with a 700-watt microwave oven with a carousel. This is a small, convenient appliance. If yours is larger, you should decrease cooking time; if smaller, increase time. If it's really bigger, wear a radiation suit.

SPICES & CONDIMENTS*

Try to purchase all these spices and condiments first (if you're in college, do this while your parents are still in town and they can help pay for them). All these things fit into a space about the size of a shoe box, so they can easily be stored under the bed or in some other out-of-the-way place. None requires refrigeration except the mayonnaise after you open it. In our shopping list section (pages 31 to 38), all of the condiments listed below will appear with a "+", meaning you already have them — if you've bought everything on this list. Incidentally, you can make healthier substitutes (low-fat mayonnaise, low-sodium soy sauce, etc.) if you wish.

The amount shown here, in the smallest available container, should last a single person about one year.

The stuff

- ☐ Apple cider vinegar
- ☐ Black pepper
- ☐ Chicken bouillon (granulated ***or*** cubes)
- ☐ Chili powder
- ☐ Cinnamon
- ☐ Cooking spray
- ☐ Cornstarch
- ☐ Curry powder
- ☐ Dried dill
- ☐ Garlic powder
- ☐ Ginger
- ☐ Hot sauce (Tabasco, or whatever)
- ☐ Italian seasoning
- ☐ Ketchup
- ☐ Mayonnaise
- ☐ Mustard
- ☐ Paprika
- ☐ Salt
- ☐ Seasoned salt (any brand)
- ☐ Soy sauce
- ☐ Vanilla
- ☐ Vegetable bouillon (granulated ***or*** cubes)
- ☐ Worcestershire sauce

* *Can they tear out this page, too?—Editor*

Folks, meet my "editor." She wants to know if you can tear this page out, too. Maybe she's figured out how to tear the other side out and leave this side in the book. This proves anybody can get a job in America.—Author

Here's what the stuff looks like

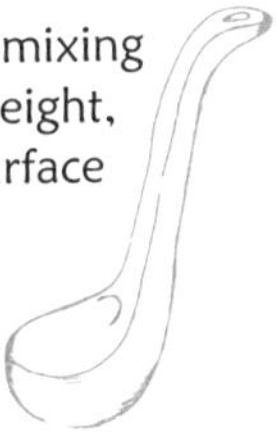

Cooking utensils made of plastic—such as ladles, mixing spoons, and measuring spoons—are inexpensive, lightweight, and come in pretty colors. They also don't scratch the surface of your bowls and plates.

Cutting boards are made of wood or heavy-duty plastic. Plastic tends to dull your knives faster. There is some controversy as to sterilization of plastic over wood. Recent tests have shown that bacteria don't grow any faster on wood than plastic, and scientists can't explain it. Some cheap wood boards can warp and discolor. Whatever you buy, wash after each use and give a quick spray of the bleach mixture described on page 70.

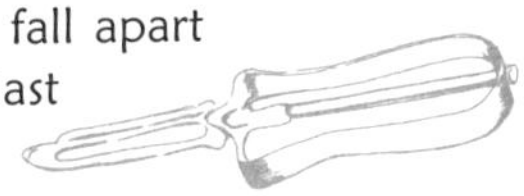

Small kitchenware like graters, peelers, and strainers should be made of stainless steel. The cheaper ones rust and fall apart quickly, so invest a little more if you can. They can last forever (or at least through several spouses).

Plates and bowls should be microwave-safe. It will be clearly marked on the package. Although there are many fine plastic products on the market, I still prefer glass. It never stains or warps, and does not scratch as easily. And they sound really neat when you drop them.

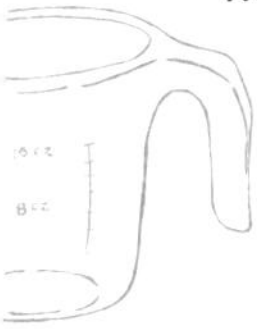

The same rule holds true for measuring ***pitchers and cups***. The glass is also easier to see through to assure correct measurements.

Vegetable brushes come in natural bristle or plastic. This time go for the plastic. It dries faster after washing, and a quick anti-bacterial spray will keep it fresh.

STUFF

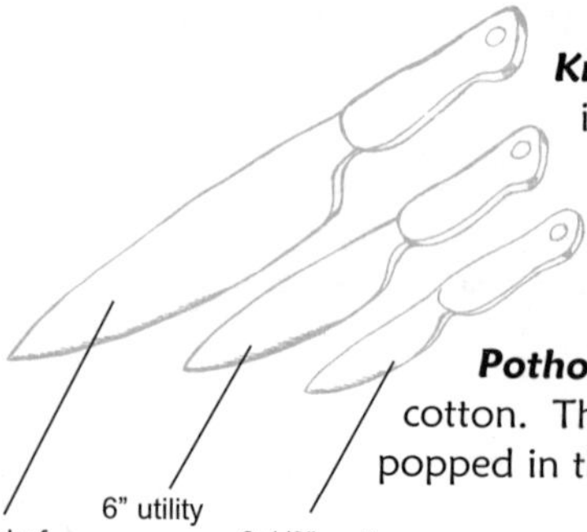

Knives are your most important kitchen investment. Always buy the best you can afford and keep them sharp. A whetstone is a good extra for you if you want to keep your knives in chef-shape.

Potholders and dish towels should be made of cotton. They are soft and absorbent and can be popped in the laundry with your bleachables.

SPICES & CONDIMENTS CRIB SHEET

Apple cider vinegar A fruity, full-bodied vinegar, great for salads. You may also use red or white wine vinegar, which is a bit more expensive. Use the white distilled stuff only for washing windows.

Black pepper This seasoning is second only to salt as the most-used seasoning. Get the smallest container they have.

Bouillon You can get bouillon in cubes or granular form. The granular is more convenient because it doesn't have to be dissolved in hot liquid first when being added to an already **hot** recipe. ***TIP:*** Beware that the Knorr products (which are excellent) make 2 cups of stock per each cube. So, use only 1/2 a cube for recipes calling for 1 cup of liquid.

Chili powder A blend of ground dried chili peppers. It comes in mild, hot, and very hot blends. Buy the kind that suits your taste. A must in Tex-Mex cooking.

Cinnamon This spice comes from the bark of a tree, but we use the ground kind in the jar for this book. It's great for baking, sprinkling on toast, or adding a lift to coffee.

Cooking spray An oil-based aerosol that keeps food from sticking to the cooking containers. It is sold in different flavors like olive oil or vegetable oil. I've used the vegetable kind in this book, but buy whatever you like.

Cornstarch A flour made from corn. I use it in the book as a thickening agent for dishes and sauces. Make sure you mix it with liquid before adding to the recipe or it will get lumpy.

Curry powder A blend of spices featuring turmeric and cumin as the major ingredients. It is used in numerous cuisines including Indian, Thai, and Middle Eastern. It ranges from quite tame to very hot. The spicy ones usually require a trip to an ethnic market to purchase.

Dill The feathery leaves of the sweet-scented plant. We use the dried kind for the book, but fresh is better. If you want to use the fresh, double the amount specified in the recipe. DON'T use the dill stems unless you require a natural laxative. You can cut it up with a knife or a pair of scissors. Add a bit to baked or boiled potatoes or a fresh cucumber.

Garlic powder This is ground dry garlic. Don't confuse this with garlic salt, which is a mixture of salt and garlic powder. You can use this in many dishes, except breakfast cereal. ***TIP:*** 1/2 teaspoon is equal to a clove of fresh garlic.

Ginger A zippy root used in baking and many oriental dishes. This book uses the ground dry version available in most markets, but if you're adventurous, 1/2 teaspoon dried is the same as about a 1/4-inch coin-shaped slice of fresh ginger.

Hot sauce A fiery blend of hot peppers and spices. In many markets there are dozens to choose from. The taste ranges from timid (Tabasco) to hotter than Hades.

Italian seasoning A pre-packaged blend of herbs including basil and oregano. There are various kinds available in the supermarket — any brand is fine.

Ketchup/catsup* A blend of pureed tomatoes and spices. The most common condiment in America *after* salsa!

Mayonnaise A whipped blend of eggs and oil. It *must* be refrigerated after opening. If you want to save a little money, the "store brands" of this product are very good.

Mustard An aromatic blend of ground mustard seeds and spices. It ranges from sweet (French's) to spicy (pass the Grey Poupon). Pick your favorite.

** I spent a couple of hours researching the difference between ketchup and catsup.—Ed.*

I know I shouldn't ask this, but what's the difference?—Auth.

The spelling!—Ed.

We have GOT to get you a hobby!—Auth.

STUFF

Salt This is, of course, the all-time most-used condiment. It comes in those large cardboard containers and packages of individual disposable shakers, which are convenient but cost a heck of a lot more. Salt substitutes are pretty good if you want to stay away from sodium.

Seasoned salt As it sounds, this is a salt product enhanced with things like onion powder, paprika, turmeric, and celery powder. Think of it as the Colonel's 11 herbs and spices and choose a brand you like.

Soy sauce A dark, rich, salty liquid made from soy beans. A necessity in oriental cooking.

Vanilla Real vanilla comes as a bean or an extract. This book uses the liquid extract. Do not buy **imitation** vanilla — it does *not* taste or cook the same way, and it isn't any cheaper. Add a bit of this to your cola or coffee for a sweet change.

Worcestershire sauce A savory blend of vinegar, molasses, garlic, anchovies, onions, and tamarinds, along with some other stuff like water. It's great to use on meats, grilled foods, and rice.

The Menus

FRIDAY
SATURDAY
SUNDAY
LUNCH
LEFTOVERS
MONDAY
SNACKS
TUESDAY
DINNER
WEDNESDAY
NOVEMBER
PIZZA
LEFTOVERS
CHICKEN
TACOS

Although this book is not limited to inexperienced cooks, menu planning and efficient use of food is a learned skill for those who want to go that route. For those who don't have the skill, or who need some help, I've outlined four weeks of ideas for you. These menus provide a reasonably healthy alternative to the peanut-butter-crackers-and-raman-noodle diet that many small families and singles slip into.

The menus will provide you with many meal ideas that don't need to be cooked (or eaten) in any specific order. We all know a good breakfast is the start of a good day, but breakfast can be pizza or fried rice and dinner can be scrambled eggs. It *is* important that you add as many fruits and raw vegetables as you want, along with milk, juices, and plenty of water. These will provide you with the kind of balanced diet that I would serve my family and will allow you to operate at peak performance.

You may make any substitution you would like to adapt these recipes to your lifestyle. Ground or cubed chicken or turkey may be substituted for all recipes calling for beef or pork with no changes to the recipes. Vegetarian substitutes, made with soy and tofu, may be substituted for things like ground meat, bacon, hot dogs, and whatever else is appropriate. In most cases, frozen vegetables may be used instead of fresh. (Yeah, we all know fresh is best — if you can, do!) Canned veggies are usually a poor substitute in taste and quality, but convenience and necessity may be more important to you.

Most of the recipes serve only one or two people, but there will be leftovers . . . so you should have plenty of body fuel each week. And you can always double or triple the numbers if the need arises.The meals are also planned in a way that maximizes the use of the food you bought that week. For example, if you buy 1/2 pound of fresh spinach, it's used two different ways (and days) in servings of 1/4-pound each.

The weekly menus and recipe sections begin with the easiest recipes and progress into pretty gourmet (but easy to make!) stuff. If you want a challenge, start in the back of each recipe section. If you want a painless way to learn some basic cooking techniques, follow the plan.

Week One

Sunday

Yo-Bananas
Mermaid Medley
Steamed spinach
Pita Parmesan

Monday

Oatmeal with milk and sugar
Cheese and tomato pita
Vegetable soup
Sprout salad

Tuesday

Raspberry Fool
Tuna salad sandwich*
Tomato-cheese soup
Green salad with dressing

Wednesday

Shredded wheat and bananas
Veggie tortilla pizza
Black beans and rice
Tomato salad

Thursday

Hard-cooked eggs with salsa
Pita bread
Buddha's Private Idaho
Spinach salad with egg

Friday

Egg salad sandwich
Chicken soup with fried noodles
Dinner-in-a-jacket
Carrot sticks with dill dip

Saturday

Fake cappuccino
Quesadillas
Black bean salad
Sliced tomatoes

*** Whoa! Why do some of these start with capital letters, and some don't?—Auth.**

Elementary, my dear Author. If they are a given name, it's capitalized. If it's generic, you use lower case.—Ed.

You must lead a very interesting life.—Auth.

Week Two

Sunday

Scrambled eggs
Bacon
Late Night Burger
Garden salad

Monday

BLT
Egg drop soup
Tuna melt
Cucumber salad

Tuesday

Cinnamon pita
Gazpacho
Spicy stuffed peppers
Homemade tortilla chips

Wednesday

Grape-Nuts cereal with berries
Porsche Potatoes
Phat Meatballs
Pasta

Thursday

Orange slush
Basic chicken salad sandwich
Chilly Chicken
Vegetable salad

Friday

Bagel with cream cheese
Veggie stew
Garlic roll
BBQ beef sandwich

Saturday

Cheese grits
Chicken 'n' Dumplin's
Snappy beans
College coffee cake

Week Three

Sunday

Ham and cheese omelet
Garlic bread
Creamy ziti bake
Romaine salad

Monday

Oatmeal with berries
Spanish rice
Oriental chicken salad
Krispy Kritters

Tuesday

Shredded wheat with peaches
Sweet and sour pork (or chicken)
Rice
Green salad with oriental dressing

Wednesday

Yo-Yo Yogurt
Tuna Fruity
Hot Dogs Hungary
Tomato salad with onion

Thursday

Bagel with peanut butter
Wings en Fuego
Celery and carrots
Blue cheese dressing

Friday

Potless Breakfast
Stuffed peppers with chicken
Pea soup
Dinner roll

Saturday

Ham and cheese pita
Lemony Chicken
Pasta
Apple crisp

Week Four

Sunday

Egg burrito
Pasta sauce
Micro-Pasta
Garlic bread

Monday

Banana Cow
BBQ chicken wings
Chili
Warm tortillas

Tuesday

Rice cereal with raisins
Pizza Presto
Beef stew
Dinner roll

Wednesday

Fruit salad
Sloppy Joans
Iceberg salad
Kung Fu Wings

Thursday

Oatmeal with raisins
Taco Smells
Guacamole
Refried beans

Friday

Cheese bagel
Meat loaf
Smashed potatoes
Apple of Your Black-Eyed Peas

Saturday

Frittata
Latin Pizza
Picadillo
Black beans and rice

The Shopping

You can't cook without food and you can't save any time, energy, or money if you don't do this chore with a battle plan. Grocery stores are some of the most intimidating places on earth. They seal the fruit in plastic so you think you **must** buy six, when you only need two. They sell Brussels sprouts in two-pound bags, like every meal is Thanksgiving dinner. Pork chops are displayed for a family of six.

Well, you can fight back!

- Ask the produce manager to break the packages.
- Tell the meat guy you need 1/4 pound of beef or *two* chicken breasts (or even one!). They are usually happy (or at least required by management) to do this.
- Buy your cheese at the deli counter so you can get the exact amount you need.
- Shop in stores that allow you to squeeze the peaches as well as the Charmin.
- Buy the smallest quantity possible in cereals and breads — *because there are no bargains if you throw half out because it gets stale.*

"Store brands" of dry cereal can be found on the bottom shelf of many markets packaged in plastic bags. They taste great and can be substituted for any name brands. Store brands of most canned goods and frozen foods are excellent.

If you follow the menus, the shopping lists provided are designed for food carryover from week to week. This will reduce food costs and waste, take advantage of the limited space in kitchenless housing, and make shopping and eating quicker and easier for you. Many of the things you bought in the first week will last throughout the menu cycle.

If you're not on the menu plan, each recipe clearly states all the food you will need for that meal. Just write down the amount and kinds of food you need, brace yourself, and head for the market.

You won't have to buy items marked with a "+" if you've stocked the condiments listed on page 14/16.

And, remember, you can tear out the shopping list if you want to.

Week One

Produce

- ☐ 4 bananas
- ☐ 6 tomatoes
- ☐ 1 package mixed greens ***or*** 1 head lettuce
- ☐ 6 scallions (also called green onions)
- ☐ 2 baking potatoes
- ☐ 1 onion
- ☐ 1/2 pound fresh spinach
- ☐ 1 package carrots

Dairy

- ☐ 1 quart milk
- ☐ 8 ounces cheddar ***or*** Monterey Jack cheese
- ☐ 1 dozen eggs
- ☐ 8-ounce package Parmesan cheese
- ☐ 8-ounce container vanilla yogurt
- ☐ 8-ounce container raspberry yogurt
- ☐ 8-ounce container sour cream
- ☐ 1 pound butter ***or*** margarine

Poultry, meat and fish

- ☐ Two 6-ounce cans tuna

Dry goods

- ☐ 1 pound long-grained rice
- ☐ ⁺1 package vegetable bouillon cubes ***or*** granules
- ☐ ⁺1 box cornstarch
- ☐ 1 pound sugar
- ☐ 1 small box of oatmeal
- ☐ 1 small box of shredded wheat cereal
- ☐ Instant coffee

Breads

- ☐ 1 package flour tortillas
- ☐ 1 package pita bread (the 4-inch size)

Canned goods

- ☐ 1 can bean sprouts
- ☐ 4-ounce can mushroom stems and pieces
- ☐ 1 can condensed tomato soup
- ☐ 1 can ready-to-serve chicken broth ***or*** ⁺bouillon cubes ***or*** ⁺granules
- ☐ 1 can black beans
- ☐ 1 can (package) chow mein noodles
- ☐ 10-3/4-ounce can condensed cream of mushroom soup
- ☐ 15-ounce jar salsa
- ☐ 1 jar sliced jalapeño peppers

Frozen foods

- ☐ 16-ounce bag mixed frozen vegetables

(continued)

Week One-cont.

Spices and condiments

- ☐ +Garlic powder
- ☐ +Cooking spray
- ☐ +Seasoned salt (any brand)
- ☐ +Salt and pepper
- ☐ +Mayonnaise
- ☐ +Mustard

} buy the smallest size you can get

Week Two

Produce

- ☐ 2 onions
- ☐ 4 plum tomatoes
- ☐ 3 scallions (also called green onions)
- ☐ 1 zucchini
- ☐ 1 summer squash
- ☐ 1 potato
- ☐ 1 pint berries
- ☐ 2 cucumbers
- ☐ 1 green pepper
- ☐ 1/4 pound green beans

Dairy

- ☐ 1 quart orange juice
- ☐ 4 ounces cream cheese
- ☐ 1/4 pound sliced provolone cheese

Poultry, meat and fish

- ☐ 1 pound chopped beef (***or*** chicken)
- ☐ 2 skinless, boneless chicken breasts
- ☐ 1/2 pound bacon
- ☐ 1/4 pound deli roast beef

Dry goods

- ☐ 1 box Grape-Nuts cereal
- ☐ 8 ounces thin spaghetti
- ☐ Small box oatmeal (not instant)
- ☐ Small box quick grits
- ☐ Small box biscuit mix

Breads

- ☐ 1 bagel
- ☐ 2 dinner rolls
- ☐ 1 package burger rolls

Canned goods

- ☐ 1 bottle chili sauce (found near the ketchup)
- ☐ 1 can whole green chilies
- ☐ 1 can vegetable broth
- ☐ 10-1/2-ounce can ready-to-serve chicken broth
- ☐ 6-ounce can tuna
- ☐ 1 can black beans
- ☐ 1 bottle barbeque sauce
- ☐ 6-pack of 5.5-ounce cans V-8 ***or*** tomato juice

(continued)

Week Two-cont.

Spices and condiments

- ☐ ⁺Cornstarch
- ☐ ⁺Soy sauce
- ☐ ⁺Worcestershire sauce
- ☐ ⁺Hot sauce (your choice)
- ☐ ⁺Dried dill (in the spice section)
- ☐ ⁺Apple cider vinegar

Week Three

Produce

- ☐ 2 peaches
- ☐ 2 apples
- ☐ 1 pint berries (any kind — but get fresh for this week's menu)
- ☐ 1 lemon
- ☐ 4 green peppers
- ☐ 2 scallions (also called green onions)
- ☐ 2 onions
- ☐ 1 cucumber
- ☐ 3 tomatoes
- ☐ 1 head romaine lettuce *(see page 92)*
- ☐ Stalk celery *(see page 86)*

Dairy

- ☐ 8-ounce vanilla yogurt
- ☐ 8-ounce cream cheese
- ☐ 4 slices American cheese
- ☐ 4 ounces cheddar cheese

Poultry, meat and fish

- ☐ 1/4 pound ground beef
- ☐ 2 chicken breasts *(see* ***NOTE*** *on page 70)*
- ☐ 1/2 pound (any kind of boneless) pork or chicken breasts
- ☐ 1 package hot dogs
- ☐ 1/2 pound deli ham
- ☐ 12 chicken wings

Dry goods

- ☐ 16-ounce box ziti pasta
- ☐ Small box crispy rice cereal
- ☐ 8-ounce package of broad egg noodles

Breads

- ☐ 1 bagel
- ☐ 1 loaf French bread*
- ☐ 1 package pita bread
- ☐ 1 dinner roll

(continued)

THE SHOPPING

* *Question: What's the difference between French bread and Italian bread?—Ed.*

Answer: Oh, about 20 minutes by train. Har, har. Hey, that killed them at chef's school. But seriously folks, use whatever. I've even made this with frankfurter rolls in a pinch.—Auth.

And she says I don't have a life!—Ed.

Week Three-cont.

Canned goods

- ☐ 1 box raisins (any size you think you can finish)
- ☐ 6-ounce can tuna
- ☐ 1 small jar green ***or*** black olives *(see page 98)*
- ☐ 1 jar peanut butter
- ☐ 8-ounce can pineapple chunks
- ☐ 1 can condensed split pea soup
- ☐ 1 bag miniature marshmallows
- ☐ Blue cheese dressing

Spices and condiments

- ☐ ⁺Ginger
- ☐ ⁺Paprika
- ☐ ⁺Italian seasoning

} buy the smallest size you can get

Week Four

Produce

- ☐ 1 lime
- ☐ 1 banana
- ☐ 1 cup fruit salad (fresh from the salad bar ***or*** you make ***or*** canned)
- ☐ 4 potatoes
- ☐ 1 avocado
- ☐ 6 scallions (also called green onions)
- ☐ 1 cucumber
- ☐ 2 green peppers
- ☐ 2 tomatoes
- ☐ 1 head iceberg lettuce *(see page 92)*
- ☐ 2 onions

Dairy

- ☐ 1 quart milk
- ☐ 8 ounces sour cream
- ☐ 4 ounces mozzarella cheese

Poultry, meat and fish

- ☐ 3 pounds ground beef
- ☐ 2 chicken breasts *(see* ***NOTE*** *on page 70)*
- ☐ 1/2 pound stew beef
- ☐ 24 chicken wings

Dry goods

- ☐ 16-ounce box spaghetti
- ☐ 1 package taco shells

Breads

- ☐ 1 bagel
- ☐ 1 dinner roll
- ☐ 1 package pita bread
- ☐ 1 package tortillas
- ☐ 1 package hamburger rolls

Frozen foods

- ☐ 1 package frozen black-eyed peas (can also be canned)

(continued)

Week Four-cont.

Canned goods

- ☐ 4-ounce can mushrooms
- ☐ 28-ounce can crushed tomatoes
- ☐ 1 can refried beans
- ☐ 1 small bottle apple juice
- ☐ Chocolate syrup
- ☐ 4-ounce can tomato sauce
- ☐ 14-ounce can peeled, chopped tomatoes
- ☐ 16-ounce can kidney beans
- ☐ 4-1/2-ounce can chopped green chilies
- ☐ 15-ounce can black beans

Spices and condiments

- ☐ +Chili powder } smallest size
- ☐ +Curry powder } smallest size
- ☐ Salsa

THE SHOPPING

The Recipes

Because I know you only want to eat and don't really want to learn to cook, these recipes have been devised to feed you fast with little clean-up and minimum equipment. Most of them can be cooked and consumed before the pizza delivery would even arrive!*

You'll find no fancy cooking terms, no exotic ingredients. Yet you'll be able to create a variety of good fast food that will feed you healthier than the burger joint. Take-out food is expensive and eating out becomes a chore after a few weeks. These recipes allow you to eat everything from burgers to Thai food, some from the microwave, some even not.

The recipes are arranged by *categories* and not *meals* because most of us haven't eaten a "traditional" breakfast, lunch, dinner, and a snack since the third grade. You don't need to cook or eat anything at any particular time, although you might want to save some of the more complicated meals for a leisurely weekend, vacation time, or a hot date.

You'll find ethnic food, Mom-style home cooking, pizza, sandwiches, and even party tips. Throughout these pages, preparation help and hints will be opposite or near the recipes where they apply. You shouldn't have to look too far to find out how to cook whatever it is you want to cook.

The format allows you to check off each step of the preparation and is written in short concise sentences that even a pre-med student or CPA could understand. This is NOT your mother's cookbook!

* *Yeah, but what if he's cute?—Ed.*

Oh...the pizza guy. *There's* a great catch!—Auth.

Publisher's note: Any reference to specific gender in this book is for convenience only, and should not be read as any of the genders currently roaming this planet. Nor do we mean to disparage pizza (or any other kind of) delivery personnel, pre-med students, or CPAs, many of whom have gone on to become substantial members of the community — financially, we mean. We are a politically correct, gender-sensitive, equal-opportunity, recycling-aware, hyphen-overusing, and all-around nice company just trying to be humorous and make a buck.

How to Boil H_2O

and other classic recipes

How to feed yourself with a cup and a spoon (without begging)

Five-star chefs know there are only a few ways to cook even the most exotic food: boil, bake, saute, fry, and broil. If you read this chapter you will have twenty percent of all cooking methods mastered. When you have completed this group of recipes I guarantee that you will never starve or miss a hot meal. If you add fruit, raw vegetables, and bread and cereal products, you have nearly a balanced diet.

Here's how the recipes work:

Boiled Water

Makes one serving

Things you need:

1-cup measure

Food you need:

Water

Way to make it:

- ☐ Measure 1 cup water into 1-cup measure
- ☐ Microcook on HIGH for 3 minutes

HINT: Use this master recipe for all the variations following.

Okay, onward and upward we go to our Kitchenless™ Adventure!

Quick Coffee

Makes one serving

Food you need:

1 cup boiled water *(see page at left ☜)*
1 teaspoon instant coffee
Optional: milk, sugar, cinnamon, vanilla extract, chocolate syrup

Way to make it:

- ☐ Add 1 teaspoon instant coffee to boiled water
- ☐ Add ***optional*** ingredients, as desired

English Breakfast Drink

Makes one serving

Food you need:

1 cup boiled water *(see page at left ☜)*
1 tea bag
Optional: sugar and lemon ***or*** milk and sugar

Way to make it:

- ☐ Add 1 tea bag to boiled water
- ☐ Allow to rest for 3 minutes
- ☐ Remove tea bag
- ☐ Add ***optional*** ingredients as desired

HINT: To zip up your tea:
- ☐ Add a slice of orange and some honey to basic tea.
- ☐ Add a slice of apple and lightly sprinkle with cinnamon on top.
- ☐ Try brown sugar and a slice of fresh ***or*** canned peach.

Dirty talk

It's very important that you clean up as you cook and wash dishes in an organized fashion. That means every meal! If you can get a significant other (or when you have children*), you may have them do this chore for you, but right now it's your problem.

If you are cooking and living in the same small room, it won't be long before you have more dirty dishes than sitting space, so take my advice . . . I've been there.

Make sure you have a garbage can with a tight-fitting lid. Line it with a plastic bag because it's easier to tie up a bag and toss it than to empty and wash a can. The plastic bags the grocer packs your food in make dandy trash can liners and are free.

Use a coffee can or attractive crock to store your cooking utensils. It doesn't take up much space and keeps them all handy. A clean dish towel placed flat on the floor can act as a dish drainer. There are also some well-designed folding drainers that can be stashed in a closet after use.

** Now about that pizza guy...—Ed.*
Geez, what a slut!—Auth.

Broth Master Recipe

Makes one serving

Things you need:

1-cup measure
1 teaspoon

Food you need:

1 cup water
1 teaspoon granulated bouillon ***or*** 1 bouillon cube *(see page 19)*

Way to make it:

- ☐ Measure 1 cup water into cup
- ☐ Microcook on HIGH for 3 minutes
- ☐ Stir in 1 teaspoon granulated bouillon ***or*** 1 bouillon cube until dissolved

HINT: You can use vegetable, beef, chicken, ***or*** fish bouillon.
Add cooked leftover pasta *(see page 47)*, vegetables, meat, or fish for a great meal. You can also top with packaged or leftover chow mein noodles.

Pasta math

You should buy pasta in 8-ounce packages. Although dried pasta does not go "bad," it ***can*** go stale and even gets bugs in some parts of the country.

TIP: If you *must* buy 1-pound boxes, you'll have to figure out the math, but here's an easy way to determine a typical (2-ounce) portion from an 8-ounce box:

If a whole 8-ounce box feeds 4 people, half that will serve 2.* Put your finger in the box and divide it in half. Now take the half you have left over and divide with your finger again. Voila . . . 2 ounces.

Pasta for non-math majors

Or, if you have a quarter-dollar handy, 2 ounces of spaghetti standing up on a quarter coin is about one serving.

* *Duh.—Ed.*

Will you wait a minute . . . I'm not finished yet!—Auth.

Single Serving Micro Pasta

Makes one serving

Things you need:

1-quart measuring pitcher

Food you need:

3 cups water
2 ounces dry pasta

Way to make it:

- ☐ Bring water to boil in a 1-quart glass container by cooking on HIGH power for 7 minutes
- ☐ Add pasta to water (***NOTE:*** If you use long spaghetti, break it in half)
- ☐ Microcook on HIGH for 7 minutes
- ☐ Drain into strainer over sink

A pasta tip Mom would never give you!

This is a *real* tip I learned as a young bride. I would, of course, never share it with my Mom, who always undercooked or overcooked her pasta. But I am pleased to say my own children have mastered this technique since childhood.

When you think the pasta is almost done, remove one piece carefully from the cooking water and throw it against a kitchen cabinet or wall. If it sticks, it's ready. **This does not work for manicotti or lasagna, however.**

Like white on rice, or brown or wild*

White rice is the grain with the hull and bran layers removed. It *does* lose some of its nutrients in this process, like white flour does. And it's almost flavorless, so it takes on the nature of the dish with which it is served, which is what you want sometimes. It looks pretty and is the kind I have used for all the recipes in this book.

Brown rice is the whole grain with only the outer husk removed. Thus, it has more nutrients. Brown rice also has a nutty flavor and chewy texture, but it *does* take longer to cook than white rice, so if you make this substitution in the recipes, increase cooking time by about 2 minutes and test for doneness by biting into a grain.

Wild rice is not rice at all — it comes from a marsh grass. Wild rice tastes very good, but it sometimes needs extensive washing and picking over and is expensive, so we don't use it in this book.

Instant rice is processed and partially cooked. It's more expensive, doesn't look or taste as good, doesn't save you all that much time, and therefore isn't used here.

Rice comes in long-, medium-, and short-grained varieties. Short is used for baking and sushi, medium doesn't show up much in the markets, so use long-grained as all-purpose.

** I have absolutely no idea what this means.—Ed.*

Don't worry, our readers are smarter than you are. It's called a simile, as in "The phone is, like, ringing."—Auth.

Rice

Makes three servings

Things you need:

1-quart measuring pitcher
1-cup measure
Fork

Food you need:

1 cup rice
2 cups water

Way to make it:

- ☐ Place 1 cup of rice and 2 cups of water in your 1-quart container
- ☐ Microcook, uncovered, on HIGH for 10 minutes
- ☐ Fluff with a fork before serving

Rice to the Rescue

This recipe serves **three**, but you are only one. You can't invite friends in for leftover rice, but boy, can you use it for fill-in dinners.

RICE WITH LEFTOVER ANYTHING

Things you need:

1-quart bowl　　Plastic wrap　　Fork

Food you need:

1 cup leftover rice
1 egg
1/4 cup leftover cooked veggies
1/4 cup leftover meat, chicken, ***or*** tofu

Way to make it:

- ☐ In a 1-quart bowl, scramble an egg with your fork
- ☐ Mix with 1 cup rice
- ☐ Add 1/4 cup leftover cooked veggies
- ☐ Add 1/4 cup leftover meat, chicken, ***or*** tofu
- ☐ Cover with plastic wrap
- ☐ Microcook on HIGH for 2 minutes

UNFRIED RICE

To 1 cup of rice and veggies (in other words, start with the above recipe), add 1 Tablespoon of soy sauce (that's about 3 packets of left-over brown liquid from the Chinese take-out*) and a sprinkle of ginger and garlic powder. Toss and give the dish a quick spray of oil. Microcook, uncovered, on HIGH for 2 minutes.

** Hey, more chances to meet guys!—Ed.*

I thought you were doing so well with the pizza guy?—Auth.

Anthony. His name is Anthony. And I'm just doing some research, that's all.—Ed.

Oh, that's what you call it.—Auth.

THE RECIPES

Fast Food Faster

quicker than the drive-thru

How to grate cheese

I know you can buy cheese already grated in nice little packages. This is fine if your trust fund check came in on time. Otherwise, this stuff costs more, molds quicker, and you have no control over quality. So buy a grater. This step takes about 15 seconds.

A four-sided (box) grater is wonderful because it lets you choose what size cheese sprinkles you want. A flat, single-sided model is available and takes up less space. Use the grater for semi- and hard cheese only. The soft ones will turn into a mushy mess. For all you need to know about cheese, check out page 138.

Use the side with the big holes to grate the less aged cheeses, like cheddar or Monterey Jack. Use the side with the little holes to grate Parmesan or Romano.

Pizza pointers

Tortillas make perfect pizza bases. You can invent your own pizza by adding whatever leftovers you have on top and sprinkling with cheese to hold it all together.

Then just pop it in the microwave on HIGH for 1 minute.

Pizza Presto

Makes four slices

Things you need:

Grater
Fork
2 pieces of paper towel
Glass pie plate

Food you need:

1 flour tortilla
1/4 cup spaghetti sauce *(buy it in a jar or see the recipe on page 189)*
1/2 cup shredded cheese — mozzarella, provolone, ***or*** cheddar *(see page at left ☜)*

Way to make it:

- ☐ Grate 1/2 cup of cheese with your grater
- ☐ Pierce tortilla several times with a fork
- ☐ Place a tortilla between 2 sheets of paper towel
- ☐ Microcook on HIGH for 1-1/2 minutes
- ☐ Transfer tortilla (not towels) to pie plate
- ☐ Spread 1/4 cup of sauce on top, leaving about 1/2 inch free around the edge
- ☐ Sprinkle with 1/2 cup of grated cheese
- ☐ Microcook on HIGH for 45 seconds until the cheese melts
- ☐ Cut into quarters and serve

How to chop

Things you need:
Cutting board — Knife*

Carrots
Peel or scrape the carrots, then put on a cutting board and cut in half lengthwise. Place flat side down and cut in half lengthwise again. This will give you four pieces. Line them up on your board and cut across them into pieces as small as you can without straining yourself.

Celery
Wash a rib of celery (for a fascinating discussion on the anatomy of celery, quickly turn to page 86). Cut the discolored ends off. Slice lengthwise 3 times, but leave a 1-inch part attached at the base. Now chop vertically across the long slits to the thickness desired.

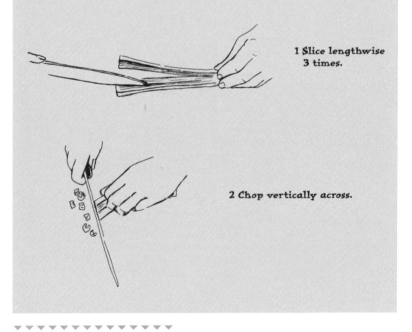

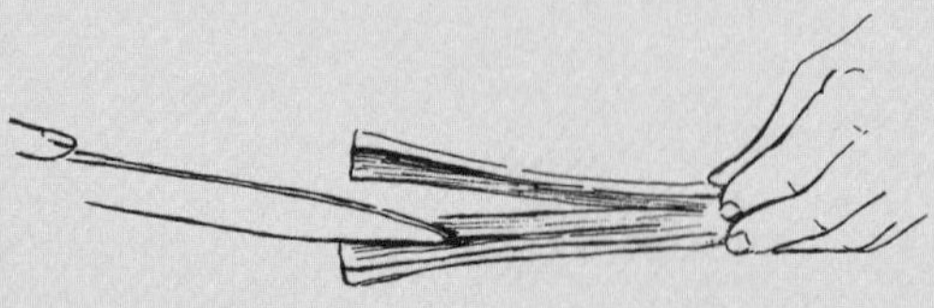
1 Slice lengthwise 3 times.

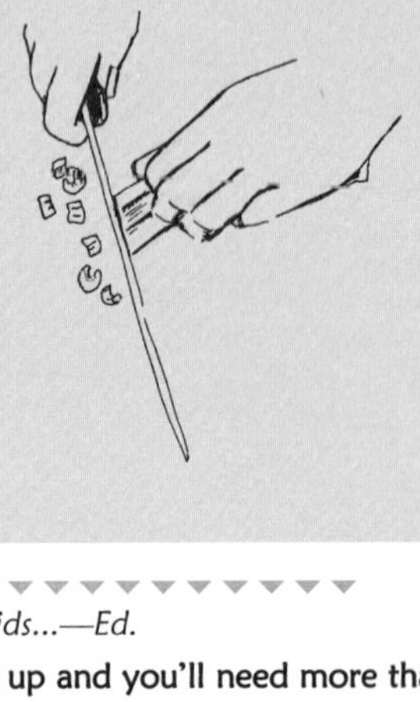
2 Chop vertically across.

* *Band-Aids...—Ed.*

Keep this up and you'll need more than a Band-Aid.—Auth.

THE RECIPES

A green pepper

Wash the green pepper. Cut the ends off the pepper, remove and discard seeds. Cut through vertically to create a rectangle. Run the knife horizontally along the inside to remove the membrane (which can be very bitter). Slice into 1/4-inch strips. Turn the cutting board 1/4 turn and slice strips again, creating a diced pepper. Easy!

An onion

Whack the ends off the onion and remove the peel. Slice in half. Place the flat side down on your cutting board and slice ***horizontally*** several times. Be careful of your fingers. Turn the onion 1/4 turn and slice vertically. Repeat with the other half. WOW! Chopped onion.

HINT: You can chop a whole onion, pop it into a freezer bag or wrap tightly in plastic wrap, and just take out the amount you need for cooking. This is very convenient and speeds prep time and clean up. It works great for peppers too, **but celery gets soggy!** And it applies to cooked dishes only.

A potato

Peel the potato if you wish, using a vegetable peeler. Remove the "eyes" if there are any. It's just like the onion above. Cut the potato in half lengthwise. Place it flat side down on your cutting board and slice it 3 times horizontally. Turn it a 1/4 way around and slice it several times.

A scallion (green onion)

Wash the scallion. Place on a cutting board and slice diagonally into 1/4-inch strips.

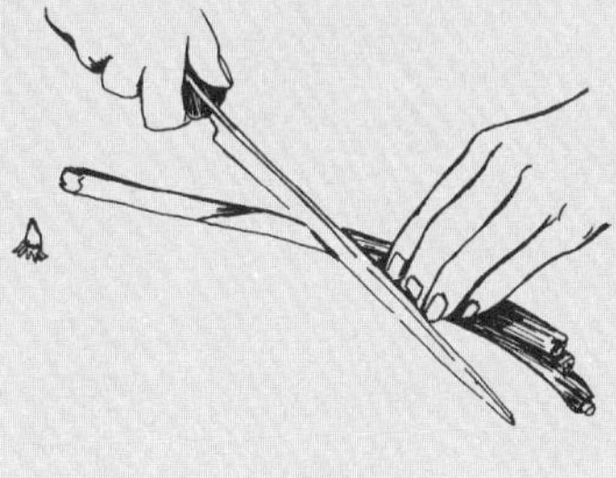

Cut ends off, the slice scallion diagonally.

(continued)

THE RECIPES

A tomato

This is also just like the onion and the potato. Wash the tomato. On the cutting board, slice the tomato in half horizontally, yadida yadida yadida.

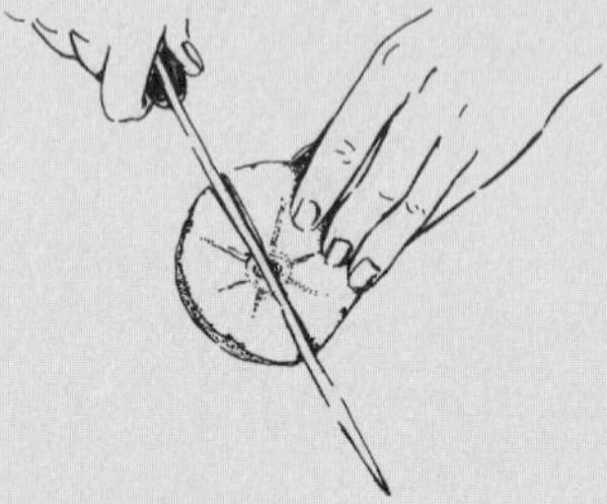

1 Slice tomato in half.

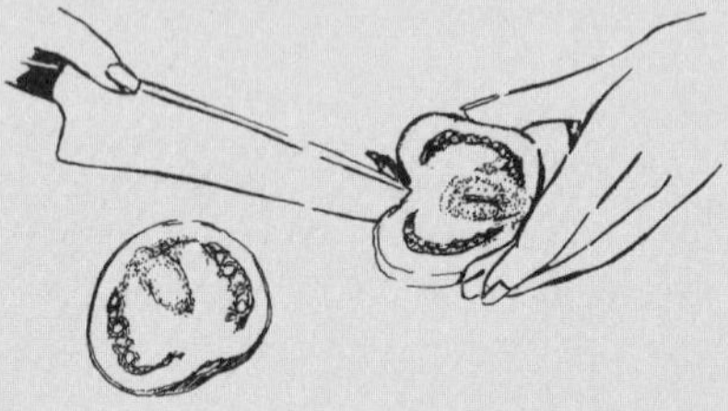

2 Remove core.

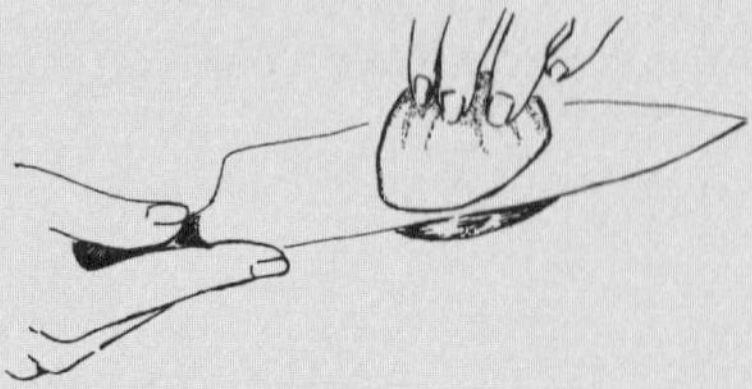

3 Slice tomato several times horizontally.

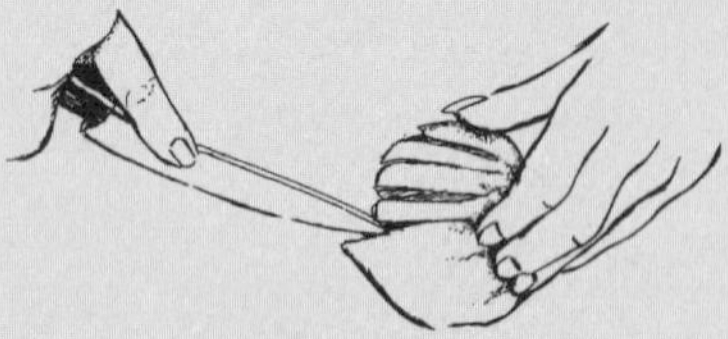

4 Turn tomato on side and slice several times vertically.

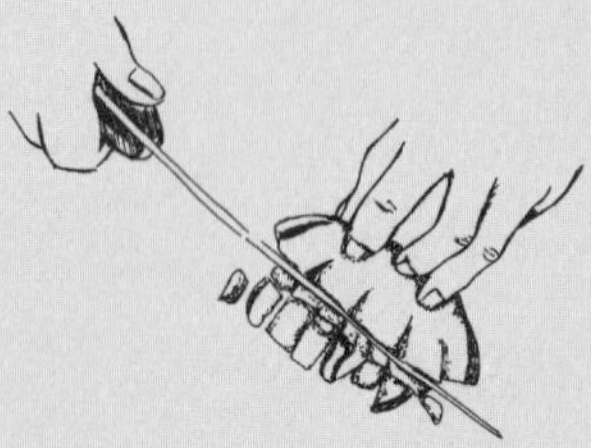

5 Chop as shown for diced tomato.

Jalapeño peppers

Don't even think about it. Buy them sliced and chopped in nice, safe little jars. That is, unless you want to worry about wearing gloves, getting the stuff in your eyes, on your privates, and generally going through the tortures of the damned because you spread the pepper oil all over the place. Man, this stuff's BAD.

Veggie Pizza

Makes 4 slices

Things you need:

Grater
Fork
Can opener
2 pieces of paper towel
Glass pie plate

Food you need:

1/2 cup coarsely shredded cheese — mozzarella, provolone, ***or*** cheddar *(packaged **or** see page 52)*
1 small tomato, chopped (it's over there ☞)
1 chopped scallion *(see page 55)*
1 Tablespoon canned mushrooms
1 flour tortilla
1 Tablespoon of any leftover vegetables you have on hand, chopped up

Way to make it:

- ☐ Grate 1/2 cup cheese with the coarse side of your grater
- ☐ Chop 1 small tomato
- ☐ Chop scallion
- ☐ Open can of mushrooms
- ☐ Pierce tortilla several times with a fork
- ☐ Place tortilla between 2 sheets of paper towel
- ☐ Microcook on HIGH for 1-1/2 minutes
- ☐ Transfer tortilla (not towels) to pie plate
- ☐ Top tortilla with chopped tomato, scallion, and 1 Tablespoon mushrooms
- ☐ Add any chopped leftover vegetables you wish
- ☐ Sprinkle with 1/2 cup grated cheese
- ☐ Microcook on HIGH for 47 seconds until cheese melts
- ☐ Cut into quarters and serve

** Why do I need this recipe when things are going so well with Anthony?—Ed.*
Uh, believe me, *you'll* need it.—Auth.

THE RECIPES

Latin Pizza

Makes four slices

Things you need:

Grater
1-cup measure
Cutting board
Knife
Can opener
Fork
2 pieces of paper towel
Glass pie plate
Tablespoon

Food you need:

1/2 cup shredded Monterey Jack cheese *(packaged **or** see page 52)*
1 chopped scallion *(see page 55)*
1 Tablespoon refried beans
1 flour tortilla
1 Tablespoon salsa
1 Tablespoon guacamole *(see page 135)*
1 Tablespoon sour cream
Optional: Jar of sliced jalapeño peppers

Way to make it:

- ☐ Grate 1/2 cup Monterey Jack cheese with grater
- ☐ Chop 1 scallion
- ☐ Open a can of refried beans
- ☐ Pierce a tortilla several times with a fork
- ☐ Place the tortilla between 2 sheets of paper towel
- ☐ Microcook on HIGH for 1-1/2 minutes
- ☐ Transfer tortilla (not towels) to pie plate
- ☐ Top tortilla with 1 Tablespoon refried beans, the chopped scallion, 1 Tablespoon salsa (and ***optional*** jalapeño peppers)
- ☐ Sprinkle with 1/2-cup grated Monterey Jack cheese
- ☐ Microcook on HIGH for 47 seconds until cheese melts
- ☐ Remove from oven
- ☐ Dollop guacamole and sour cream on top
- ☐ Cut into quarters and serve

Hot Ham-and-Cheese Pita

Makes one sandwich

Things you need:

Knife
Cutting board
Paper towel

Food you need:

1/4 pound deli ham
2 slices cheese
1 pita bread, sliced to make pockets *(see page 124)*
Mustard

Way to make it:

- ☐ Slice pita through the middle to make 2 pocket sides
- ☐ Spread mustard inside each pocket
- ☐ Fold over 1 slice of cheese and place in each pocket
- ☐ Fold over 1 slice of ham and shove inside the cheese slice
- ☐ Place the stuffed pitas on a paper towel and microcook on HIGH for 30 seconds until cheese is melted

Hamburger patty cake

TIP: Most markets carry fresh or frozen chopped beef in pre-made, 1/4-pound patties. This is very convenient for the Kitchenless™ cook. If the recipe calls for 1/2 pound, you simply pull out 2 patties and pop the rest back into your tiny freezer.

OR . . .

Buy 1 pound of ground meat, divide it into 4 pieces, and shape your own patties. Place a square of wax paper between the patties and store them in the freezer, wrapped in something plastic.

Late Night Burgers

Makes one serving

Things you need:

Teaspoon
Glass pie plate

Food you need:

Hamburger patty *(see **TIP** at left ☜)*
Salt
Pepper
Garlic powder
2 teaspoons of barbeque sauce
Hamburger roll

Way to make it:

- ☐ Place pre-shaped hamburger patty on plate
- ☐ Microcook on HIGH for 2 minutes
- ☐ Drain juice from plate
- ☐ Add a sprinkle of salt, pepper, and garlic powder, along with 1 teaspoon BBQ sauce
- ☐ Return to microwave and microcook on HIGH for 2-1/2 minutes
- ☐ Remove from oven
- ☐ Dab on 1 teaspoon BBQ sauce
- ☐ Place on roll

HINT: You don't need me to tell you what to load on top of a burger. In case you didn't know, though, the famous "secret" sauce is merely Thousand Island dressing (*see page 107* — or just adding a quick dollop of mayo and ketchup will save you about a million dollars in development costs and market research).

Bacon tips

You may use either (regular) pork, turkey, or vegetarian bacon for all recipes calling for bacon. They cook and taste nearly the same, but the turkey has less fat, and the vegetarian none at all.

Bacon will keep in the refrigerator in a tightly closed container for about two weeks. But it freezes well and will keep for up to two months.

Cooked bacon can be kept tightly wrapped and refrigerated for five days. I suggest you cook a half-pound on a weekend, then fill in with BLT lunches *(see page 64)* or chop into bacon omelets later in the week. To re-heat, place two pieces of bacon on a double-folded paper towel and microcook on HIGH for 10 seconds.

Microwave Bacon

Makes 1/2 pound of bacon

Things you need:

9-inch microsafe pie plate
Fork
4 pieces of paper towel

Food you need:

1/2 pound sliced bacon

Way to make it:

- [ ] Line the glass pie plate with four layers of paper towel
- [ ] Place slab of bacon on towels (no need to separate into pieces)
- [ ] Cover bacon with one paper towel
- [ ] Microcook on HIGH for 5 minutes
- [ ] Now, separate into pieces with fork
- [ ] Re-cover with paper towel
- [ ] Microcook on HIGH for 5 more minutes
- [ ] Remove from oven
- [ ] Transfer to clean paper towel to drain off fat
- [ ] For extra crispy, return desired number of pieces to microwave and cook on HIGH for 1 minute

TIP: To crumble bacon, microcook it extra crispy and mush it up in your hand(s). If it's not crispy enough, use your knife or, much better, a pair of scissors.

BLT

Makes one sandwich

Things you need:

Knife
Cutting board
Paper towel
Teaspoon

Food you need:

1 small tomato
3 lettuce leaves
3 pieces ***cooked*** bacon *(see page 63)*
2 pieces of bread (rye tastes great)
1 teaspoon mayonnaise

Way to make it:

- [ ] Slice 1 small tomato
- [ ] Rinse 3 lettuce leaves and pat dry with paper towel
- [ ] Place 3 pieces of ***previously cooked*** bacon on a folded piece of paper towel on microwave oven floor
- [ ] Microcook on HIGH for 10 seconds
- [ ] Spread bread with 1 teaspoon mayonnaise
- [ ] Add tomato slices, lettuce, and bacon
- [ ] Top with remaining piece of bread and press down

Basic Egg Salad

Makes one serving

Things you need:

Knife
Cutting board
Soup bowl
Tablespoon
Fork

Food you need:

1 hard-cooked egg *(see page 120)*
1 Tablespoon onion, chopped *(see page 55)*
1 Tablespoon mayonnaise
Dash of seasoned salt
Bread ***or*** pita

Way to make it:

- ☐ Coarsely chop (***or*** mash with a fork) the egg
- ☐ Place in bowl
- ☐ Add 1 Tablespoon chopped onion and one Tablespoon mayonnaise
- ☐ Mix to blend
- ☐ Add seasoned salt
- ☐ Place on bread ***or*** pita with lettuce and tomato, if desired

Gourmet eggs: Add 1/4 teaspoon of dried dill

Huevos Pronto: Omit the mayo and onion and add 1 Tablespoon of salsa

TIP: Any leftovers of egg and tuna salads are great mixed together.

How to drain tuna (or anything else in a can)

Open the can, but leave the top in place — don't totally remove it. Turn the can upside down over a sink, pressing down on the lid with your fingers. In seconds you have perfectly drained tuna.* Throw out the top and use the nice dry meat in your recipe.

This is a great method for draining beans or any other canned vegetables, too.

* *Which is pretty good if you're draining kidney beans.—Ed.*
See what crawls in when you don't change the roach traps? —Auth.

Basic Tuna Salad

Makes two servings

Things you need:

Can opener
1-quart bowl
Fork
Tablespoon
Teaspoon

Food you need:

6-ounce can of tuna, drained *(there's how ☜)*
2 scallions, chopped ***or*** 2 Tablespoons chopped onion — that's about an inch-thick chunk *(see page 55)*
1 Tablespoon mayonnaise
1 teaspoon mustard
2 slices of any kind of bread ***or*** pita

Way to make it:

- ☐ Drain the tuna
- ☐ Crumble tuna into a bowl, breaking up the pieces with a fork
- ☐ Add 2 chopped scallions
- ☐ Add 1 Tablespoon mayonnaise and 1 teaspoon mustard
- ☐ Mix well with your fork
- ☐ Spread with your fork on bread ***or*** stuff it in a pita that has been cut through the middle to make 2 pockets
- ☐ Add lettuce and tomato, if desired

TIP: And to make it less than basic, here are some alternatives to chop up and mix in: onion, chow mein noodles, pickles, apples, celery, relish, or cucumber. Then add some condiments: salt, pepper, curry powder, dill, celery powder, or seasoned salt.

SON/DAUGHTER OF TIP: Any leftovers of tuna and egg salads are great mixed together.

Tuna Melt

Makes two servings

Things you need:

Fork
Knife
Cutting board
2 pieces of paper towel
Plate
Tablespoon

Food you need:

1/2 cup basic tuna salad *(see page 67)*
One 8-inch tortilla
3 slices tomato, any thickness you like
3 slices cheese

Way to make it:

- ☐ Pierce the tortilla in several places with your fork
- ☐ Slice the tomato to any thickness you like
- ☐ Place the tortilla between 2 sheets of paper towel and microcook on HIGH for 1-1/2 minutes
- ☐ Transfer the tortilla (not towels) to a plate
- ☐ With a Tablespoon, top with tuna mixture and the tomato slices and cover with the cheese slices
- ☐ Microcook on HIGH for 45 seconds

BBQ Beef Sandwich

Makes one sandwich

Things you need:

Knife
Cutting board
1-cup measure
Tablespoon

Food you need:

1/4 pound deli roast beef
1/4 cup barbecue sauce
1 slice onion
Hamburger roll

Way to make it:

- ☐ Slice 1 piece of onion
- ☐ Separate into rings
- ☐ Put onion rings and 1/4 cup barbecue sauce into a 1-cup microsafe measure
- ☐ Microcook on HIGH for 1 minute
- ☐ Cut the beef into thin strips
- ☐ Stir into sauce mixture with your Tablespoon
- ☐ Microcook on HIGH for 1 minute until just hot
- ☐ Spoon onto hamburger roll

Chicken safety tips

Carefully wash and pat dry on a paper towel all chicken before cooking. Chicken carries a bacteria (salmonella) that can easily contaminate other food. It's a good idea to chop all your vegetables and prepare* all other ingredients that require the cutting board before you place the chicken on the board.

Wash all utensils and the board in hot soapy water after use, and spray with an anti-bacterial solution.

TIP: An excellent anti-bacterial spray can be made by mixing 1/4 cup chlorine bleach with 3/4 cup water. Put in a well-marked spray bottle and use on your board after washing. This is much less expensive than — and equally as effective as — store-bought sprays.

NOTE: When I talk about using a chicken breast, I am talking about 1/2 of a whole breast. When you buy chicken breasts, remember they are single breasts that come in pairs, just like the human ones. It usually comes as one big piece of meat joined at the breastbone with a strip of white cartilage in between, but it is still considered two breasts! So cut the breast in half at the joining point and you have two, not one, for the money!

*** Or, as we say in the business, prep.—Auth.**

Well E-X-C-U-U-U-S-E ME!!—Ed.

Poached Chicken Breasts

You can poach several pieces of chicken all at one time and then use the cooked meat as needed all week.

Things you need:

Glass pie plate
Paper towel
Plastic wrap
Teaspoon
1-cup measure
Knife

Food you need:

2 boneless skinless chicken breasts *(look over there ☞)*
1/4 teaspoon seasoned salt
1/4 cup water

Way to make it:

- ☐ Wash 2 skinless, boneless chicken breasts; dry with paper towel
- ☐ Place on your glass pie plate
- ☐ Sprinkle with 1/4 teaspoon seasoned salt
- ☐ Add 1/4 cup water to bottom of plate
- ☐ Cover with plastic wrap
- ☐ With your knife, cut a 1-inch slit in the wrap
- ☐ Cook on HIGH for 4 minutes
- ☐ Cool and refrigerate

HINT: Some deli counters now sell cold grilled chicken breasts. They are a speedy, though expensive, way to create great salads, sandwiches, and quick meals in general.

Basic Chicken Salad

Makes one serving

Things you need:

Cutting board
Knife
Tablespoon
Teaspoon
1-quart bowl
Spoon

Food you need:

1 small (1/2 large) cooked chicken breast *(see page 71)*, cut in small pieces (about 1/2 cup), ***or*** use any chicken leftovers
2 Tablespoons chopped celery *(start with a 1/2 rib and see pages 86 & 54)*
2 Tablespoons chopped onion *(start with an inch-thick chunk and see page 55)*
1/8 teaspoon seasoned salt
2 Tablespoons mayonnaise
Bread ***or*** pita

Way to make it:

- ☐ Cut cold, cooked chicken into small pieces until you have 1/2 cup
- ☐ Chop 2 Tablespoons each of celery and onion
- ☐ Place everything in your 1-quart bowl, sprinkle with 1/8 teaspoon seasoned salt
- ☐ With your mixing spoon, mix well with 2 Tablespoons mayonnaise
- ☐ Serve on bread ***or*** pita

TIP: You can also use canned chicken or turkey for this recipe.*

* *You can also use Spam.—Ed.*

Spam. That's why I'm the chef and you go after pizza guys.—Auth.

Publisher's note: Please see previous Publisher's note on page 40.

Garlic Rolls

Makes one roll

Things you need:

Paper towel

Food you need:

1 dinner roll
Garlic powder
Cooking spray

Way to make it:

- [ ] Spray dinner roll with cooking spray
- [ ] Place on a piece of paper towel on the oven floor
- [ ] Sprinkle with garlic powder
- [ ] Microcook on HIGH 15 seconds

Garlic Bread

Makes one loaf

Things you need:

2 paper towels
Knife
Cutting board

Food you need:

1 loaf of French (or Italian or Cuban or whatever) bread
Cooking spray ***or*** butter ***or*** margarine
Garlic powder
Parmesan cheese

Way to make it:

- ☐ Place 2 pieces paper towels on bottom of oven
- ☐ Slice bread in half horizontally, like you were going to make a hero
- ☐ Liberally spray cut sides with cooking spray ***or*** spread with butter ***or*** margarine
- ☐ Dust with garlic powder
- ☐ Microcook on HIGH for 2 minutes
- ☐ Sprinkle with Parmesan cheese

TIP: For a step up, also sprinkle with your Italian seasoning.

Warm Tortillas

Makes two tortillas

Things you need:

Paper towel
Fork

Food you need:

2 tortillas

Way to make it:

- ☐ Dampen (NOT dripping wet!) 2 pieces of paper towel with water
- ☐ Put one piece on the microwave oven floor
- ☐ Pierce the tortillas with the fork in several places
- ☐ Place the tortillas on top of the paper towel
- ☐ Cover with the other damp towel
- ☐ Microcook on HIGH for 1-1/2 minutes

Homemade Tortilla Chips

Makes a bunch

Things you need:

Paper towels (as many as you need to cover the floor of your microwave)

Food you need:

A bunch of soft corn tortillas (however many you want)
Cooking spray

Way to make it:

- ☐ Spray all the tortillas with cooking spray
- ☐ Arrange 4 tortillas at a time, oil side up, on paper toweling in microwave
- ☐ Microcook on HIGH for 2 minutes
- ☐ Remove the tortillas and the paper towel
- ☐ Return the tortillas to the microwave, placing them directly on the oven floor
- ☐ Microcook on HIGH for 2 minutes more

NOTE: *Tortillas should be crisp but will not be brown*

- ☐ Repeat process for the rest of the tortillas
- ☐ Break into pieces

HINT: This is a great way to use up less-than-fresh tortillas.

Pita Parmesan

Makes one serving

Things you need:

Knife
Cutting board
Custard cup
Microsafe plate
Teaspoon
Tablespoon

Food you need:

1 whole wheat ***or*** white pita bread
2 Tablespoons butter ***or*** margarine
1/2 teaspoon garlic powder
2 Tablespoons grated Parmesan cheese
1/2 teaspoon Italian seasoning

Way to make it:

- ☐ Cut the pita bread into quarters
- ☐ Separate the tops and bottoms to make 8 triangles
- ☐ With your Tablespoon, mix 2 Tablespoons butter ***or*** margarine and 1/2 teaspoon garlic powder together in a custard cup
- ☐ Microcook on HIGH for 1 minute
- ☐ Place 2 Tablespoons of Parmesan cheese and 1/2 teaspoon Italian seasoning into the custard cup and stir the butter/herb mixture with the Tablespoon
- ☐ With the Tablespoon, spread a small amount of the cheese mixture onto each pita triangle
- ☐ Arrange pita triangles on plate
- ☐ Microcook on HIGH for 1 minute
- ☐ Eat right away

Florida Iced Tea

Makes four 8-ounce glasses

(This is so simple and cheap you'll never buy instant again)

Things you need:

1-quart pitcher

Food you need:

1 quart of water
4 tea bags
Optional: 8 teaspoons sugar ***or*** the equivalent in sweetener

Way to make it:

- ☐ Fill a 1-quart measure with water
- ☐ Add tea bags
- ☐ Place in a sunny spot and go to class or tennis or watch "Days of Our Lives"*
- ☐ When you return (about an hour), remove the tea bags, add ***optional*** sweetener, pour over ice ... ahhhh

OPTION: Reserve 1 cup of water. Place in a bowl and add as much sugar as you like. Microcook on HIGH for 5 minutes. Add to tea for a SWEET drink.

TIP: May be refrigerated, covered, for 3 days.

* *Or call the pizza guy.—Ed.*

Will somebody rent her a videotape or something?—Auth.

Dos Esses*

(Soups & Salads)

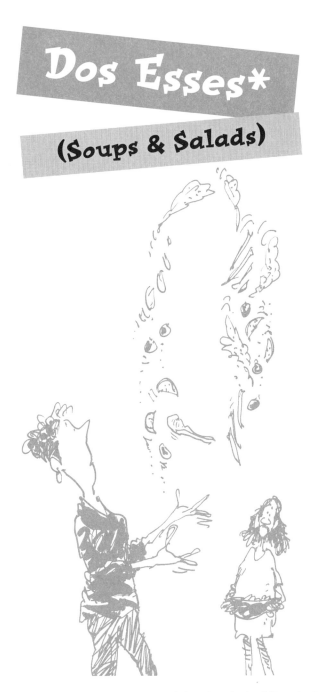

* ***Publisher's note:*** Now, the writer and the editor had a "discussion" about this chapter heading. The writer thought the combination of Spanish and English to read "Two Esses" for **S**oup and **S**alads was debilitatingly witty and clever. The editor just didn't get it.

How to set a table

For those of you who have never been food servers, the fork goes on the left, knife and spoon on the right. This is easy to remember — if you are right-handed, you must reach across the plate to pick up your fork. The glasses go on the right, along with the knife and spoon. The napkin, neatly folded, goes on the left with the fork. Of course, you could stuff it in a glass and pretend you are at a fancy restaurant, or embrace it with a too, too divine napkin ring and sup with the Queen.*

* If you want more information on proper table service (and manners), I recommend — despite the unfortunate title — ***Tiffany's Table Manners for Teenagers*** by Walter Hoving, published by Random House. Throw away the dust jacket and destroy the title with Magic Marker. (Yeah, yeah, it's a trademarked name.)—Auth.

Egg Drop Soup

Makes two servings

Things you need:

Teaspoon
1-cup measure
Mixing spoon
Can opener
Tablespoon
1-quart bowl
Fork
Another cup
Cutting board
Knife

Food you need:

2 teaspoons cornstarch
1/4 cup water
One 14-ounce can ready-to-eat (***not*** condensed) chicken broth
2 Tablespoons soy sauce
1/8 teaspoon garlic powder
1 egg
1 scallion, chopped *(see page 55)*

Way to make it:

- ☐ Mix 2 teaspoons of cornstarch with 1/4 cup water in cup (use the teaspoon to mix)
- ☐ Using your mixing spoon, combine 1/8 teaspoon garlic powder, 14-ounce can ready-to-eat chicken broth, 2 Tablespoons soy sauce, and cornstarch mixture in your 1-quart bowl
- ☐ Microcook on HIGH for 5 minutes
- ☐ Beat egg with fork in a cup
- ☐ Chop scallion
- ☐ Remove broth from oven
- ☐ Pour egg slowly into bowl while stirring the soup lightly with the fork
- ☐ Sprinkle with scallion for that restaurant look and taste

Chicken Soup with Fried Noodles

Makes one serving

Things you need:

Can opener
1-cup measure
Serving bowl
Tablespoon

Food you need:

1 can ready-to-eat (not condensed) chicken broth
1 Tablespoon chow mein noodles (from a can, package, or take-out leftovers*)

Way to make it:

- ☐ Pour 1 cup of ready-to-eat (not condensed) chicken broth into serving bowl
- ☐ Microcook on HIGH for 2 minutes
- ☐ Garnish with 1 Tablespoon chow mein noodles

HINT: Add chopped scallions, leftover canned mushrooms, or chopped hard-cooked egg to beef up this dish.

** I have lots of leftovers now.—Ed.*

I know this is a mistake, but why is that?—Auth.

I took your advice. Lots of Chinese food — it's healthy, delicious, and . . .—Ed.

. . . I know, and the delivery guy is even cuter than Anthony.—Auth.

Hey, how'd you...—Ed.

Can we just get on with it?—Auth.

Vegetarian Vegetable Soup

Makes three servings

Things you need:

Can opener
Cutting board
Knife
1-quart bowl
1-cup measure
Teaspoon
Mixing spoon
Soup bowls
Optional: Grater

Food you need:

One 14-ounce can ready-to-eat (***not*** condensed) vegetable broth ***or*** 2 vegetable bouillon cubes ***or*** 2 teaspoons of vegetable bouillon granules *(see page 19)* dissolved in 2 cups of water
2 small, fresh tomatoes, chopped *(see page 56)*, saving the juice
The juice from the tomatoes
3/4 cup frozen mixed vegetables
1/2 teaspoon seasoned salt
2 Tablespoons grated Parmesan cheese, fresh *(see page 52)* ***or*** packaged
Optional: 1/2 cup cooked pasta (something small, like shells) *(see page 47)*

Way to make it:

- ☐ Microcook soup on HIGH for 2 minutes
- ☐ Chop two small tomatoes
- ☐ Add 3/4 cup frozen mixed vegetables, the chopped tomatoes and juice, and 1/2 teaspoon seasoned salt to soup
- ☐ Microcook on HIGH for 5 minutes
- ☐ With mixing spoon, ladle into soup dishes and add 1 Tablespoon of grated Parmesan cheese per serving

Gazpacho

Makes one serving

Things you need:

Blender *(check out the blender tips on page 112)*
Teaspoon

Food you need:

Large handful of garden salad *(see page 96)*
One 5.5-ounce can of V-8 ***or*** tomato juice
1/2 teaspoon Worcestershire sauce
Hot sauce

Way to make it:

- ☐ Put a big handful of leftover garden salad in the blender
- ☐ Add a 5.5-ounce can of V-8 ***or*** tomato juice
- ☐ Add 1/2 teaspoon Worcestershire sauce
- ☐ And a dash or two of hot sauce
- ☐ Blend on HIGH until smooth
- ☐ Eat right away or keep chilled for later

HINT: For elegance beyond words, add a Tablespoon of cut up cucumber, peeled or not. Cut 'em up like the carrot on page 54.

Tomato-Cheese Soup

Makes two servings

Things you need:

Can opener
1-quart bowl
Plastic wrap
Optional: Grater
1-cup measure
Cutting board
Knife
Mixing spoon

Food you need:

One 10-ounce can condensed tomato soup
One 10-ounce can water
1/2 cup grated cheddar ***or*** Monterey Jack cheese *(packaged or see page 52)*
Optional: 1 scallion, chopped, ***and/or*** 4 slices of jalapeño pepper *(see pages 55 & 56)*

Way to make it:

- ☐ Empty contents of a can of tomato soup into your 1-quart bowl
- ☐ Add one can of water; stir
- ☐ Cover with plastic wrap and microcook on HIGH for 5 minutes
- ☐ Grate (or use packaged) 1/2 cup cheddar cheese (about 2 ounces)
- ☐ Chop 1 scallion
- ☐ Add cheddar cheese to soup
- ☐ Microcook on HIGH for 1 minute
- ☐ Stir with mixing spoon
- ☐ Garnish with scallions and peppers, if desired

Celery vocabulary

Celery is like lettuce — it grows in a bunch. The whole bunch is called a head or sometimes a stalk. Each individual rib makes up the head, but to further confuse you, these are also sometimes called stalks. So, here's the vocab for the purpose of our recipes.

A **stalk** of celery is the whole head or bunch.

A **rib** of celery is one of the long pieces that make up the stalk.

HINT: 1/2 of a celery rib makes about 2 Tablespoons chopped.

Thick-As-Pea Soup

Makes two servings

Things you need:

Cutting board
Knife
2-1/2-quart bowl
Tablespoon
Can opener

Food you need:

1 carrot
1 rib of celery *(see page at left ☜)*
1/2 small onion
1 Tablespoon butter ***or*** margarine
1 can ***condensed*** split pea soup
1 can water
1 hot dog

Way to make it:

- ☐ Chop carrot, celery, and 1/2 onion into small pieces *(see pages 54 & 55)*
- ☐ Put vegetables in a 2-1/2-quart bowl with 1 Tablespoon butter ***or*** margarine
- ☐ Microcook on HIGH for 4 minutes
- ☐ Add 1 can of ***condensed*** split pea soup and 1 can of water
- ☐ Slice the hot dog into 8 pieces
- ☐ Add the hot dog pieces to the vegetable soup mixture and stir with the Tablespoon
- ☐ Microcook on HIGH for 5 minutes

Raisin tips

Remember when you were little and Mom used to tuck those little boxes of raisins in your lunch box? They tasted sweet, were good for you, and were so much fun to eat from those cute packages.

Well, it's time to buy them for yourself again. One small box can be used in the Tuna Fruity *(next page ☞)*, sprinkled over your oatmeal, or mixed into your yogurt.

The small packaging is more convenient for use in the recipes and keeps the raisins from forming that mysterious sugary ball that seems to happen when you open a whole big box and don't use it right away. It also means they don't need refrigeration and the sugar ants won't feast on them if left unattended.

Tuna Fruity

Makes two servings

Things you need:

1-quart bowl
Fork
Tablespoon
Knife
Mixing spoon
Teaspoon
Cutting board

Food you need:

3 Tablespoons mayonnaise
1 teaspoon curry powder
1 can tuna, drained *(see page 66)**
1 scallion, chopped *(see page 55)*
1 small box (1/4 cup) raisins
1/2 cup chopped apple ***or*** peach
Salt and pepper to taste
Optional: Pita bread ***or*** salad greens *(see page 91)*

Way to make it:

- ☐ With your mixing spoon, mix together 3 Tablespoons mayonnaise and 1 teaspoon curry powder in your 1-quart bowl
- ☐ Drain the tuna
- ☐ Crumble the tuna into the mayonnaise mixture, breaking up the pieces with a fork
- ☐ Chop 1 scallion and 1/2 cup fruit (if you use an apple, core it — *see page 192* — then treat as an onion — *page 55*); if you want to use a peach, cut it in half, remove the pit, and treat it like the apple
- ☐ Add to the tuna mixture
- ☐ Add 1 small box (1/4 cup) raisins
- ☐ Mix well
- ☐ Cut the pita in half to stuff with the tuna mixture ***or*** . . .
  . . . serve on salad greens ***or*** eat alone

HINT: This may also be made with canned ***or*** cooked chicken ***or*** turkey.

* *I made this with Spam. It was great.—Ed.*

I'm beginning to think there is a relationship between eating Spam and the killing off of brain cells.—Auth.

Publisher's note: Oh, great. Now we get sued by Spam.

Lettuce spray*
How to clean vegetables

We know all sorts of nasty chemicals are sprayed on our food to make them pretty and tasty. **All** vegetables (even organic) must be thoroughly washed before eating, especially if they are to be served raw. Even if you're into natural food, dirt, bugs, and people sweat may all be unwanted — if organic — additives.

You should *scrub* all root vegetables — like potatoes, carrots, and parsnips — under cold water with a vegetable brush. This removes dirt from handling and also rinses away much of the chemicals.

Lighter-skinned vegetables — such as squash, celery, and tomatoes — should be *rinsed* and can be carefully cleaned with a brush as well.

You have the option of peeling cucumbers and carrots. I like the texture better after peeling, but that's my personal choice — some like the color and "crunch" of the peel. To remove any lingering dirt, rinse with cold water after peeling.

Salad greens should be rinsed and drained before adding dressing. Nothing is worse than soggy salad!† Before you begin to cook, take the amount of greens you need, wash them, and simply place in your strainer to drain in the sink. Toss the greens occasionally . . . they should be dry by the time you're ready to serve.

Try to buy **pre-washed** spinach. It's a bit more expensive but worth it. Getting rid of spinach grit can take several washings. When you take it out of the package, "refresh" it by quickly running under cold water and draining before serving as a salad.

Both fresh and canned sprouts also benefit from a brief cold shower before serving. Just rinse and drain.

*** Wow — more great food humor!—Auth.**

OK, when do we start?—Ed.

† *Not even creeping underwear?—Ed.*

Around the greens

Many of you may only be familiar with two kinds of greens. Those found on a golf course and iceberg lettuce.* You are really missing something!

In all of these recipes, a combination of greens really perks them up and — because we live in an era driven by convenience — this is easy to accomplish. Most markets now sell packaged mixes of various greens that range from iceberg lettuce (with a bit of chopped cabbage and carrot for color, if nothing else) to gourmet stuff loaded with field greens (like dandelions and watercress). Try them all.

The other advantage to the premixed stuff is you can pull out a handful at a time to make a single serving, seal it back up, and pop it in the 'fridge. It seems to take a month for only one person to eat a head of boring iceberg. With these handy packages you can have greater variety and more convenience.

But if you're set on making your own combinations, I have provided a list of salad greens on the next page.

HINT: Always ***break*** your greens into pieces. Don't use a knife. Breaking greens will prevent browning along the edges. Trust me.

THE RECIPES

** I'm into the kind in wallets.—Ed.*

Yeah, keep dating pizza guys.—Auth.

Oh that's old news. I'm dating Dennis now.—Ed.

Who's Dennis? Don't tell me — the Chinese delivery guy. My editor, the social climber.—Auth.

Publisher's note: . . . Oh, never mind.

Green salad stuff

Iceberg lettuce has a large round head with tightly packed leaves. It's light green in color and quite crunchy, but bland-tasting. It is great on sandwiches and stands up to thick dressings like Ranch and Thousand Island.

Romaine has a long head with dark green leaves. It has a tangy flavor and is the base of the famous Caesar Salad. Dirt collects easily in its stiff leaves. Cut off the bottom (stem end) and wash very well before using.

Boston lettuce, with its small round head, is not as tightly packed as iceberg. It has soft, delicate leaves and is used best in light salads with a clear dressing. It has a smooth, buttery flavor.

Oak leaf is usually red and resembles its name. This is a "show" green — it looks great. Wonderful and smoky, mix it with other greens to add both color and flavor to your salad.

Chicory is curly edged with an elongated stem. It has a bitter flavor and a prickly feel in the mouth. Use sparingly.

Belgian endive has a very small, elongated head of light-colored leaves. This slightly bitter green is great chopped and tossed in a salad, but even better for a base of cool chicken or tuna salad, chopped egg, or even deli chopped liver. Spoon it on and use like a cracker. Wash well first — this one is another grit hider.

Watercress is a wonderful peppery green with long stems and small dark green leaves. It is a nice spicy addition to a green salad, also a good garnish for special occasions like **Candlelight Chicken** on page 187.

Spinach can be used as a separate salad ingredient or combined with other greens. Its dark green color and toothsome texture add a nice touch to all salads. It is a real grit holder, so wash very well — several times — or buy the pre-washed kind.

Green Salad

Makes one serving

Things you need:

1-quart (**or** soup) bowl
Cutting board
Knife
Paper towel
Mixing spoon

Food you need:

One handful of salad greens *(look over to the left ☜)*
1 scallion, sliced into 1/2-inch pieces *(see page 55)*
Salad dressing *(bottled **or** see page 107)*

Way to make it:

- ☐ Wash a handful of salad greens and pat dry on paper towel
- ☐ Slice the scallion into 1/2-inch pieces
- ☐ Toss into 1-quart (**or** soup) bowl
- ☐ Pour on your favorite dressing and toss with your mixing spoon.

TIP: You can add a ton of other goodies, too *(see **TIP** on page 96).*

THE RECIPES

The $7.50 salad

There is a very upscale chop house in my town that actually charges $7.50 for the very same recipe as on that page over there ☞. Tell your friends you went to Boca Raton (yes, that *is* where the real *Saturday Night Live* Linda Richman lives) and you asked the chef for this recipe.

How to core, shred, and otherwise mangle iceberg lettuce

Hold the lettuce in both hands, core side down. Bang it hard on a counter. The core will pop right out! If this isn't enough to let out your aggression, cut the head in half along where the core used to be, place the cut side down on your cutting board, and whack away like mad with your biggest knife.* More sedate people can neatly slice through the head making nice, neat ribbons to show the teacher.

THE RECIPES

*Hey, didn't you say on page 91, and I quote, "Don't use a knife."?!—Ed.

You know, with just a little bit more effort you could be a real pain in the ...—Auth.

Publisher's note: ...kitchen, say kitchen. Oh please say kitchen.

Iceberg with Thousand Island Dressing

Makes one serving

Things you need:

Strainer
Cutting board
Knife
Plate

Food you need:

1/4 head iceberg lettuce, cored *(check it out there ☞)*
Thousand Island salad dressing *(bottled **or** see page 107)*

Way to make it:

- ☐ Core lettuce
- ☐ Rinse and drain in strainer
- ☐ Slice into four quarters
- ☐ Reserve three quarters for another salad
- ☐ Plop the remaining quarter on a plate
- ☐ Slather with Thousand Island dressing

REBELLIOUS SON/DAUGHTER OF HINT ON PAGE 91: This is the only place where it's OK to cut lettuce with a knife. When you copy what is essentially a $7.50 bowl of lettuce, you can do darn near anything you want to it.

Garden Salad

Makes one serving

Things you need:

Cutting board
Knife
Soup bowl
Mixing spoon
Strainer

Food you need:

One handful of salad greens *(see page 91)*
1/2 rib celery *(see page 86)*
1/2 carrot
1 plum tomato
Parmesan cheese
Salad dressing of your choice *(bottled **or** see page 107)*

Way to make it:

- ☐ Rinse a handful of salad greens and drain in strainer
- ☐ Cut 1/2 rib celery into 1/4-inch pieces
- ☐ Slice 1/2 carrot into 1/4-inch coins
- ☐ Cut tomato into 4 wedges
- ☐ Mix it all in a soup bowl with your mixing spoon and toss again with your favorite dressing

HINT: Make a double batch of this salad and only put the dressing on half for tonight. Keep the leftover for gazpacho tomorrow! *(See recipe on page 84.)*

TIP: You can also add a load of other things, like pieces of carrot, cucumber, celery, tomato, radishes, little squares of toast (croutons), cheese, broccoli, cauliflower, apples, oranges, pineapple, eggs, meat (like sliced packaged chicken, turkey, ham, salami, Spam,* sardines, whatever). The more junk you put in, the more it gets to be a main course — meat and cheese make it a chef's salad; fruits and cottage cheese make it a Californian.

*** How'd *that* get in there?—Auth.**
♪♩ La-dee-dah. . .♪♩—Ed.

THE RECIPES

Spinach Salad with Chopped Egg

Makes two servings

Things you need:

Cutting board
Knife
2-1/2-quart or salad bowl
1-cup measure

Food you need:

2 handfuls of spinach
1 hard-cooked egg *(see page 120)*
2 scallions
1/4 cup vinaigrette dressing *(bottled **or** see page 107)*

Way to make it:

- ☐ Carefully wash and pat dry 2 handfuls of spinach
- ☐ Tear into bite-sized pieces and place in 2-1/2-quart or salad bowl
- ☐ Cut scallions into 1/2-inch pieces
- ☐ Chop cooked egg into small pieces
- ☐ Add egg and onions to spinach and use your mixing spoon to toss with the vinaigrette dressing

TIP: You can also add sliced fresh (best) ***or*** canned mushrooms ***or*** cooked, crumbled bacon *(see page 63)* if you have them on hand.

Olive stuff*

Olives are a great snack and a big addition to tacos, pizza, salads, and sandwiches. They come in many sizes and colors and range from ultra salty to very mild.

Try to buy them in glass jars instead of cans. They will keep a long time but must be refrigerated after opening. Canned olives should be transferred to a glass jar for storage.

The supermarkets always carry the usual green and black (ripe) olives, but many of the larger chains have added exotic imports. They are deep-flavored and briny and come from all over the world. Give them a try. You'll be surprised at the different tastes and textures.

*"***You see,***" said the Author to the Editor, "**some olives are stuffed with little pieces of pimiento pepper. That's what makes this double entendre funny!**"

"*Oh,*" said the Editor to the Author.

Romaine with Cheese & Olives

Makes one serving

Things you need:

Strainer
Cutting board
Knife
Optional: Grater
1-quart bowl
Mixing spoon

Food you need:

One handful romaine lettuce, wash and break into pieces *(see page 92)*
1 chopped scallion *(see page 55)*
4 olives
2 Tablespoons white cheese such as crumbled feta **or** grated Parmesan *(packaged* ***or*** *see page 52)*
1 Tablespoon vinaigrette dressing *(bottled* ***or*** *see page 107)*

Way to make it:

- ☐ Wash romaine
- ☐ Drain in strainer in sink
- ☐ Tear into bite-sized pieces
- ☐ Chop scallion
- ☐ Toss one handful romaine, scallion, and crumbled feta ***or*** Parmesan cheese into a 1-quart bowl
- ☐ Add 4 olives — or more if you like olives
- ☐ Toss with 1 Tablespoon dressing using your mixing spoon

Tomato tip

Tomatoes should be bright, shiny, and red when you buy them. But we can't have vine-ripened tomatoes all year long. So, here's how to cheat:

Sprinkle sliced tomatoes with 1/8 teaspoon sugar. This will bring more life to them and that great sweet taste you love. Lie to your friends and tell them you had these treats flown in on the corporate jet.

Tomato Salad

Makes one serving

Things you need:

Cutting board
Knife
1-quart bowl
Teaspoon

Food you need:

1 ripe tomato
1/4 teaspoon seasoned salt
1/8 teaspoon pepper

Way to make it:

- ☐ Wash a ripe tomato. With a small, sharp knife cut the stem out of the tomato (it's the little brown thing on the top)
- ☐ Cut the tomato into 4 wedges
- ☐ Cut each wedge in half across the middle to make 8 chunks
- ☐ Place tomato in bowl and sprinkle with 1/4 teaspoon seasoned salt and 1/8 teaspoon pepper
- ☐ If you allow the salad to sit 15 minutes, it will make its own "dressing"

Veggie Salad

Makes one serving

Things you need:

1-quart bowl
Cutting board
Knife
Tablespoon

Food you need:

1 handful mixed vegetables *(see **HINT** below)*
1 scallion, sliced *(see page 55)*
1 Tablespoon salad dressing *(bottled **or** see page 107)*

Way to make it:

- ☐ Put one handful **cooked** mixed vegetables in a bowl
- ☐ Chop 1 scallion and toss into the bowl
- ☐ Toss with 1 Tablespoon of your favorite salad dressing using your Tablespoon

HINT: This is meant to use leftovers, but you can also use frozen and (in a pinch) canned veggies. If you start with frozen, just put a handful in your 1-quart bowl with a Tablespoon of water and microcook on HIGH for 1-1/2 minutes. Cool for a few minutes in the refrigerator, then proceed with the rest of the recipe.

Sprout Salad

Makes one serving

Things you need:

Strainer
1-quart bowl
Teaspoon
Tablespoon
Cutting board
Knife
Mixing spoon

Food you need:

1 cup fresh ***or*** canned bean sprouts
1 scallion, chopped *(see page 55)*
1 Tablespoon soy sauce
1/2 teaspoon sugar

Way to make it:

- ☐ Wash 1 cup of sprouts and drain in strainer
- ☐ Place the sprouts in your 1-quart bowl
- ☐ Chop 1 scallion and add to the bowl
- ☐ Add 1 Tablespoon soy sauce and 1/2 teaspoon sugar
- ☐ Toss until well coated using your mixing spoon

How to peel & slice a cucumber

Things you need:

Cutting board
Knife
Teaspoon
Optional: Vegetable peeler

Food you need:

1 cucumber

Way to make it:

- ☐ If you want to peel the cuke, use the ***optional*** vegetable peeler to remove the skin
- ☐ Cut the cucumber in half lengthwise (the long way)
- ☐ With the teaspoon, scoop out the seeds and discard
- ☐ Place the cucumber halves flat side down on the cutting board and slice to desired thickness

HINT: Thickly chopped cucumbers add a nice crunch to salads, ***or*** slice them wafer-thin as a garnish.

Cucumber Salad

Makes one serving

Things you need:

Cutting board
Knife
Strainer
1-quart bowl
Teaspoon
Tablespoon
Optional: Vegetable peeler

Food you need:

1/2 cucumber (if you like it peeled, *see over there* ☜)
1/2 teaspoon salt
1/2 teaspoon vinegar
1/4 teaspoon dried dill
1 Tablespoon sour cream ***or*** yogurt

Way to make it:

- ☐ If you like it that way, peel 1/2 cucumber with ***optional*** vegetable peeler
- ☐ Slice cucumber thinly
- ☐ Place in strainer and sprinkle with 1/2 teaspoon salt
- ☐ Let drain over a bowl or the sink while you prepare dinner
- ☐ Mix 1/2 teaspoon vinegar, 1/4 teaspoon dried dill, and 1 Tablespoon sour cream ***or*** yogurt in your 1-quart bowl
- ☐ Add drained cucumber
- ☐ Eat now or chill for several hours

Black Bean Salad

Makes one serving

Things you need:

Cutting board
Knife
Strainer
1-quart bowl
Teaspoon
Mixing spoon

Food you need:

1 canned chile pepper, finely chopped (**or** 1 Tablespoon fresh, pre-chopped)
1/2 can black beans, rinsed and drained *(see page 66)*
1 scallion, chopped *(see page 55)*
1/2 tomato, chopped *(see page 56)*
1/4 teaspoon garlic powder
Hot sauce
2 Tablespoons vinaigrette dressing *(bottled* **or** *cast thine eyes eastward ☞)*

Way to make it:

☐ Finely chop 1 canned green chile pepper (**or** use 1 Tablespoon pre-chopped), 1 scallion, and 1/2 tomato
☐ Rinse and drain 1/2 can of black beans
☐ Place in your 1-quart bowl and add the chopped vegetables and 1/4 teaspoon garlic powder
☐ Add a dash of hot sauce and toss using your mixing spoon with 2 Tablespoons bottled **or** homemade vinaigrette dressing

TIP: Remember to save the other 1/2 can for black beans and rice *(see the recipe on page 137)* or to add to other salads or chili.

Salad dressings

There are many great prepared dressings on the market and I'm sure you have your favorite. But homemade is easy and cheaper than the bottled stuff and will last refrigerated for months. Here's a few to try, if you've got the time.

Vinaigrette In a small jar with a tight-fitting lid, mix 1/2 cup of olive oil, 2 Tablespoons apple cider vinegar, 1/4 teaspoon garlic powder, 1/2 teaspoon salt, 1/2 teaspoon sugar, and 1/2 teaspoon mustard. Add 1 ice cube and shake until well blended. Remove what's left of the ice cube and serve.

Italian Add 1/2 teaspoon of Italian seasoning to the above ingredients.

Thousand Island In a small bowl, use your Tablespoon to stir together 1/4 cup chili sauce, 3/4 cup mayonnaise, 6 chopped olives, 1 Tablespoon chopped onion, and a dash Worchester - shire sauce.

Honey mustard In a small jar with a tight-fitting lid, mix 1/2 cup oil (vegetable, canola, safflower, whatever except olive), 2 Tablespoons apple cider vinegar, 2 Tablespoons mustard, and 2 Tablespoons of honey. Cover and shake until well blended.

HINT: The key to a professional-looking salad is to lightly dress it and toss very well to coat all the greens. You can always add more dressing if there's not enough, but a soggy mess in the bottom of the salad bowl is both wasteful and yucky looking.

Oriental Salad Dressing

Makes enough for two salads

Things you need:

Tablespoon
Teaspoon
Jar with a tight-fitting lid

Food you need:

1 Tablespoon vinegar
2 Tablespoons soy sauce
1/8 teaspoon hot sauce
1 teaspoon peanut butter
1 teaspoon sugar
1 ice cube

Way to make it:

- ☐ Add 1 Tablespoon vinegar, 2 Tablespoons soy sauce, 1/8 teaspoon hot sauce, 1 teaspoon peanut butter, 1 teaspoon sugar, and 1 ice cube to a jar with a tight-fitting lid
- ☐ Shake until blended

TIP: Use this on the oriental chicken salad *(over there ☞)* or *any* greens. It will keep refrigerated for one month.

THE RECIPES

Oriental Chicken Salad

Makes two servings

Things you need:

Cutting board
Knife
1-quart bowl
Mixing spoon
1-cup measure

Food you need:

1 cup shredded lettuce *(see page 94)*
1 cup cold **cooked** chicken, sliced maybe 1/4-inch thin *(see page 71)*
1/2 small carrot, sliced thin
1/2 cucumber, sliced thin
1 jar oriental dressing *(☞ over there)*
1/2 cup packaged chow mein noodles

Way to make it:

- ☐ Make the oriental dressing
- ☐ Cut 1 cup of lettuce in shreds with knife
- ☐ Slice cold, **cooked** chicken into thin strips to make 1 cup
- ☐ Slice 1/2 small carrot and 1/2 cucumber in thin slices
- ☐ Place everything in your 1-quart bowl and toss in the pre-made dressing using your mixing spoon
- ☐ Sprinkle 1/2 cup packaged chow mein noodles on top

HINT: You can slice the chicken easier if it's chilled.

Salad daze

Since those active and intelligent people using this book are under the pressure of time and must read wherever the opportunity presents itself (in class, at your desk, at the weekly status meeting), we are generously including an intellectual pursuit to keep your mind at its peak of performance. Salad words are hidden forward, backward, up, down, and diagonally in the grid. Loop a word, check it off the list, and feel good about yourself. Our editor has the option of dating any of the guys who send in the solution.*

Solution on page 220

H	H	D	C	R	G	H	F	D	W	C	E	M	N	D
K	S	R	R	E	D	N	E	T	H	C	T	S	Y	F
O	M	A	E	F	N	L	V	A	U	S	N	M	D	V
O	M	L	W	R	L	N	B	D	L	H	E	D	O	E
C	A	L	C	I	U	M	O	C	S	T	M	R	O	Y
K	F	O	H	G	B	R	A	I	S	Y	H	E	F	I
O	L	C	M	E	P	B	D	N	T	V	S	Y	A	T
F	A	E	L	R	B	R	O	U	I	I	I	I	N	L
V	V	N	T	A	A	I	T	T	E	K	R	A	M	H
D	O	O	G	T	L	V	A	R	U	E	U	T	B	C
S	R	E	S	E	U	M	S	I	F	R	O	D	U	A
A	W	U	D	B	I	C	T	E	I	W	N	L	R	N
L	M	N	C	N	W	N	E	N	B	B	O	I	L	I
A	A	K	S	E	L	B	A	T	E	G	E	V	P	P
D	E	L	I	C	I	O	U	S	R	E	M	M	I	S

- ☐ BETA carotene
- ☐ BOIL
- ☐ CABBAGE
- ☐ CALCIUM
- ☐ CHILLED
- ☐ COLLARD greens
- ☐ COOK
- ☐ DANDELION greens
- ☐ DELICIOUS
- ☐ DISH
- ☐ FIBER
- ☐ FLAVOR
- ☐ FOOD
- ☐ FRESH
- ☐ GOOD
- ☐ HEALTHY
- ☐ KALE
- ☐ LEAF
- ☐ LETTUCE
- ☐ MARKET
- ☐ MEAL
- ☐ MUSTARD greens
- ☐ NOURISHMENT
- ☐ NUTRIENTS
- ☐ NUTRITION
- ☐ PRODUCE
- ☐ REFRIGERATE
- ☐ SALAD
- ☐ SIMMER
- ☐ SPINACH
- ☐ STEM
- ☐ TASTE
- ☐ TENDER
- ☐ TURNIP greens
- ☐ VEGETABLES
- ☐ VITAMINS
- ☐ WASH

* Yeah, but only the first 1,000.—Ed.

Breakfast-Type Foods

Blender tips

Cleaning tip

- ☐ Fill blender 1/3 full with warm water
- ☐ Add a small amount of dish detergent
- ☐ Cover container and run for a few seconds
- ☐ Rinse and dry container thoroughly

Blender lockjaw

When you're whirling away on some food, and the blender seems to have developed lockjaw, add a bit more liquid (water is fine). It will un-jam the food and get the action started again.

Reminder

The little clear top of the blender is removable, and that's all you have to take off if you need to add a little something to the blend. It also serves as a fine measure for adding liquids 1 ounce at a time.

Raspberry Fool

Makes one serving

Things you need:

Blender
Mixing spoon
Custard cup

Food you need:

1 banana
8-ounce container of raspberry yogurt

Way to make it:

- ☐ Break the banana into 6 pieces
- ☐ Place 1 banana and one 8-ounce container of raspberry yogurt in the container of your blender
- ☐ Cover and whirl at HIGH speed until frothy
- ☐ With your mixing spoon, scoop out of the blender and into a custard cup

Orange Slush

Makes one serving

Things you need:

Custard cup
1-cup measure
Blender
Mixing spoon

Food you need:

1 egg
1 cup orange juice
1/2 cup milk
1/4 cup fresh ***or*** frozen berries

Way to make it:

- ☐ Break the egg into custard cup
- ☐ Microcook on HIGH for 30 seconds (it will not be fully cooked, but sterile)
- ☐ Put 1 cup orange juice, 1 cooked egg, 1/2 cup milk, and 1/4 cup berries in container of blender
- ☐ Cover and whirl until smooth
- ☐ With your mixing spoon, scoop the slush out of the blender into a custard cup

TIP: Despite the success of Rocky Balboa, **don't** eat raw eggs in any way, shape, or form.

Banana Cow

Makes one serving

Things you need:

Blender
1-cup measure
Tablespoon
A glass

Food you need:

1 banana
1/2 cup milk
1 Tablespoon chocolate syrup

Way to make it:

- ☐ Break banana into container of blender.
- ☐ Add 1/2 cup milk and 1 Tablespoon chocolate syrup
- ☐ Cover and whirl on HIGH until smooth
- ☐ Pour into a glass

Fake Cappuccino

Makes one serving

Things you need:

Blender
Measuring cup
Teaspoon
Tablespoon

Food you need:

3/4 cup milk
1 Tablespoon sugar ***or*** 1 package sweetener
1 Tablespoon instant coffee
1/8 teaspoon cinnamon
Ice to fill 3/4 of a glass

Optional: whipped cream of some kind (fake, real aerosol, stolen from roommate's strawberry shortcake)

Way to make it:

- ☐ Put 3/4 cup milk, 1 Tablespoon sugar (***or*** a package of sweetener), 1 Tablespoon instant coffee, and 1/8 teaspoon cinnamon in container of blender
- ☐ Whirl on HIGH until frothy
- ☐ Pour into glass over ice and top with whipped cream, if desired

Oatmeal

Makes one serving

Things you need:

1-quart measuring pitcher
Soup bowl
Mixing spoon

Food you need:

2/3 cup water
1/3 cup rolled oats (not the instant kind)
Pinch of salt

Way to make it:

- ☐ Measure 2/3 cup water into pitcher
- ☐ Add 1/3 cup rolled oats and a pinch of salt
- ☐ Microcook on HIGH for 2 minutes
- ☐ Stir and cook 47 seconds
- ☐ Add sugar and milk if desired
- ☐ With your mixing spoon, scoop out everything in the pitcher into a soup bowl*

* *I'd eat it right out of the bowl, with Dennis ♥♥♥.—Ed.*

Gee, you're just a hopeless romantic.—Auth.

Eggciting info

Buying eggs

Eggs come in different sizes and colors, just like people. I'm partial to the brown ones because they look like they have a healthy tan, but there really is no difference in "store bought" eggs by color. They also come in sizes — medium, large, extra large, and jumbo. This book has used large for all the recipes, but there is little difference in how they will perform in the recipes. Buy the ones that fit your pocketbook and appetite. If you live in the country, or are in a college that has an "Aggie school," buy your eggs from the farm. The difference in taste between really fresh and supermarket eggs is astonishing!

Storing eggs

To last longer, eggs must be refrigerated. Even though your refrigerator may come with a handy plastic egg holder, the best way to store eggs is in their original containers. Both temperature and light affect the aging process (just like humans!), so keep them quietly nested in the nice dark Styrofoam or cardboard grid they rode home in. They can keep this way for at least 2 weeks.

🡐 this is an egg

Breaking eggs

Don't ever break an egg on the edge of the cooking vessel. A piece or two of shell will drop in and then you spend 12 minutes trying to get it out with a fork.* Instead, tap the shell on the side of the counter, a sturdy glass, or the sink to crack, then open it over the bowl.

How to prevent egg-splosions

Eggs should be cooked at low temperatures for best results. This is difficult to do in a microwave — the eggs revolt and explode 3 seconds before "done" time, leaving you with a mess. Try this to prevent a disaster. Always poke the yolk several times with the tip of a sharp knife. Place a piece of plastic wrap, also with a hole poked in it, over the egg container. If your microwave has power settings, lower the number and increase cooking time by about 25 percent.

this is an egg in an anti-drug commercial ➔

* *Why bother? I just eat it. Jason doesn't mind—Ed.*

You would . . . wait a minute. Who's Jason?—Auth.

Well, remember that slush thing? I left the spoon in the blender, and when I turned it on . . . KROOSH! So I brought it in to be fixed.—Ed.

I'm beginning to get the rhythm of this now. There was Jason . . . *KROOSH?!* — Auth.

Hard-Cooked Eggs

Makes one egg

Things you need:

Cup
Knife
Plastic wrap

Food you need:

1 egg

Way to make it:

- ☐ Break 1 egg into a cup
- ☐ Pierce yolk with tip of knife
- ☐ Cover with plastic wrap
- ☐ Poke a hole in the wrap with your knife
- ☐ Microcook on HIGH for 60 seconds
- ☐ Allow to stand one minute

HINT: Add a little salsa to the egg after cooking for a spicy start to your day.

Scrambled Eggs

Makes one serving

Things you need:

Small bowl
Fork

Food you need:

2 eggs
Cooking spray

Way to make it:

- ☐ Spray bowl with cooking spray
- ☐ Break eggs into bowl
- ☐ Whip eggs with fork
- ☐ Microcook on HIGH for 1 minute
- ☐ Stir, then microcook on HIGH 45 seconds more

Additions:

1 Tablespoon of any of the following may be added ***before*** cooking:

Chopped scallion
Chopped onion
Grated cheese
Chopped mushrooms
Pieces of cream (or any) cheese
Chopped (cooked or deli meat) ham or salami or bologna or any cut up (well, commercially butchered, at least) dead animal

TIP: You might want to add a dollop of ketchup or hot sauce after cooking.

Great Omelet Variations

Any combination of the following may be added to the basic omelet on the right ☞.

- Grated cheese
- Chopped scallions
- Cooked vegetables
- Sour cream
- Cottage cheese
- Chopped ham
- Salsa
- Canned mushrooms
- Chopped tomatoes
- Italian seasoning
- Sauteed onions
- Cooked crumbed bacon
- Cooked meat **or** chicken
- Pimentos
- Jalapeño peppers *(see page 56 first)*
- Bottled red roasted peppers, chopped

Oodles of Omelets

Makes one serving

BASIC OMELET

Things you need:

1-quart bowl
Teaspoon
Tablespoon
Fork
6-inch plate
Knife
Cutting board

Food you need:

2 eggs
1 teaspoon water
Cooking spray
Optional: 2 Tablespoons filling *(look over to your left ☜)*

Way to make it:

- ☐ In a 1-quart bowl, use the fork to beat 2 eggs with 1 teaspoon water until well blended (it becomes a light-lemony color)
- ☐ Spray 6-inch plate with cooking spray
- ☐ Pour egg mixture into plate and microcook on HIGH for 2 minutes
- ☐ With the fork, loosen the edges of the egg from the plate (it will help fold it over later)
- ☐ ***Optional:*** add fillings
- ☐ Lift edge of omelet with fork and fold egg over filling
- ☐ Microcook on HIGH for 30 seconds

Pita bread tips

Keep the pitas stored in the refrigerator in the original plastic wrap. They will easily keep for two weeks.

To slice for Potless Breakfast *(over there ☞)* **or pizza** *(you can use pitas instead of tortillas in all the pizza recipes here)*, place the bread flat on a cutting board and carefully run the knife through it. Watch your fingers!

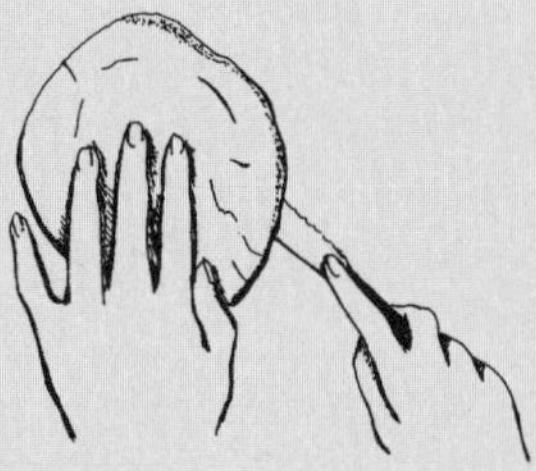

1 Lay pita flat and run knife horizontally through it.

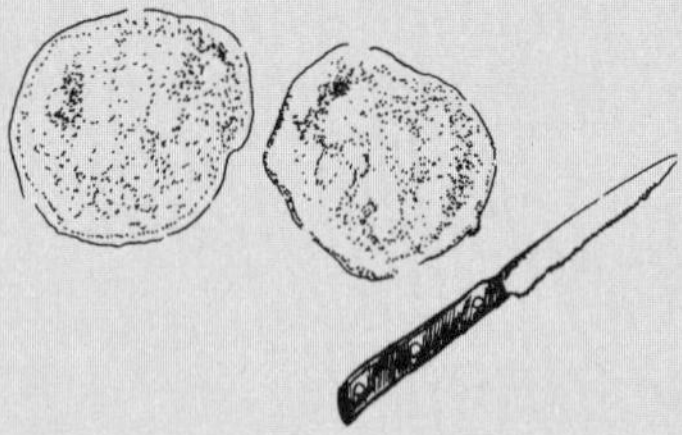

2 Separate halves.

To slice for sandwiches, cut through the bread along the middle and gently pull the center apart to create a pocket in each half for stuffing with your favorite filling.

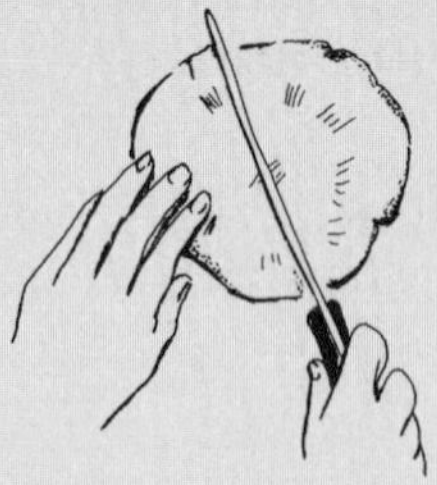

1 Cut pita in half.

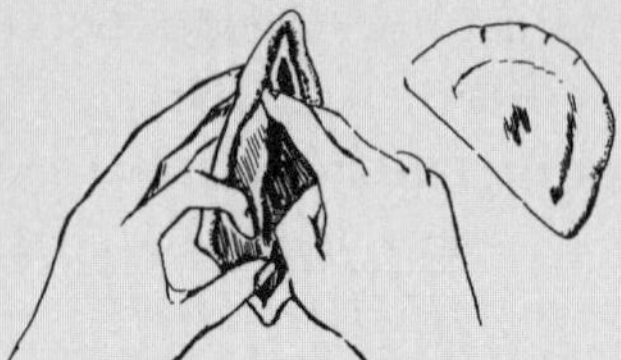

2 Gently pull sides apart.

TIP: Make Cinnamon Pita *(see page 126)* a snap by mixing 2 parts sugar with 1 part cinnamon in a clean salt shaker. You can then sprinkle it on fast and easy. Save it for other things, too, like regular toast, French toast, cream cheese, even coffee or ice cream.

Potless Breakfast

Makes one sandwich

Things you need:

Knife
Paper towel
Tablespoon

Food you need:

1 pita bread (about 4-inch size)
1 Tablespoon salsa
1 slice ham
1 slice cheese ***or*** 2 Tablespoons grated cheese
1 egg

Way to make it:

- [ ] Slice pita horizontally to create a base and top *(look over there ☞)*
- [ ] Place both on a piece of paper towel in microwave
- [ ] Spread salsa on the bottom half, top with cheese and ham
- [ ] Carefully break egg in center of base
- [ ] Pierce yolk with the tip of a knife to prevent unwanted explosion
- [ ] Microcook on HIGH for 1 minute
- [ ] Allow to rest for 1 minute (it will continue to cook)
- [ ] Top with other half of bread to make a sandwich and off you go with no dishes to wash later

Cinnamon Pita

Makes one serving

Things you need:

Fork
Teaspoon
Paper towel

Food you need:

1 pita bread
1 teaspoon sugar
1/2 teaspoon cinnamon

Way to make it:

- ☐ Prick pita all over with a fork
- ☐ Sprinkle it with 1 teaspoon sugar mixed with 1/2 teaspoon cinnamon
- ☐ Place on a paper towel
- ☐ Microcook on HIGH for 45 seconds

HINT: Life is short, check the ***TIP*** on page 124.

Egg Burrito

Makes one burrito

Things you need:

1-quart bowl
Cutting board
Knife
Paper towels
Plate
Mixing spoon

Food you need:

Cooking spray
1/2 small tomato, chopped *(see page 56)*
1 small scallion, chopped *(see page 55)*
2 Tablespoons green pepper, chopped *(see page 55)*
1/4 teaspoon garlic powder
1 raw egg, beaten
1/4 teaspoon chili powder
1 Tablespoon grated (packaged) Parmesan cheese
1/8 teaspoon each of salt and pepper
1 tortilla
Sour cream and bottled salsa

Way to make it:

- ☐ Spray bowl lightly with cooking spray
- ☐ Chop the tomato, scallion, and green pepper and add to bowl
- ☐ Microcook on HIGH for 1 minute
- ☐ Remove from oven and add egg, 1/4 teaspoon garlic powder, 1/4 teaspoon chili powder, 1 Tablespoon grated (packaged) Parmesan cheese, 1/8 teaspoon salt, and 1/8 teaspoon pepper
- ☐ Microcook on HIGH for 1 minute, stirring after 45 seconds
- ☐ Lay a tortilla between two sheets of damp paper towel
- ☐ Place tortilla flat on dish in microwave
- ☐ Microcook on HIGH for 15 seconds
- ☐ Remove paper towel and place tortilla on plate
- ☐ Spoon mixture on top of tortilla and roll up
- ☐ Top with salsa and sour cream*

** Or just plop it all on top before you roll it up.—Ed.*

I was going for presentation here.—Auth.

Oh, excuse me. Let me frame my egg burrito.—Ed.

Frittata

Makes two servings

Things you need:

Knife
Cutting board
Pie plate
Small bowl
Fork
Tablespoon

Food you need:

Cooking spray
1 small onion, chopped } *(see page 55)*
1 potato, diced }
1/4 of a bell pepper (any color), chopped (about 2 Tablespoons) *(this is also on page 55)*
3 eggs

Way to make it:

- ☐ Spray pie plate with cooking spray
- ☐ Chop onion and place in pie plate
- ☐ Microcook on HIGH for 1 minute
- ☐ Chop 1/4 of a bell pepper to yield about 2 Tablespoons and dice the potato
- ☐ Add peppers and potato to onions in pie plate
- ☐ Microcook on HIGH for 3 minutes
- ☐ With the fork, beat eggs in small bowl
- ☐ Add eggs to vegetables in pie plate and stir to combine
- ☐ Microcook on HIGH for 3 minutes or until eggs look as firm as you like them
- ☐ Eat right away

TIP: This dish is great in the micro because the eggs do not brown. And as we learned in chef's school, browned eggs are burned eggs.

Yo-Yo Yogurt

Makes one serving

Things you need:

Strainer
Custard cup
Tablespoon

Food you need:

A couple of Tablespoons fresh ***or*** frozen berries (any kind)
1/2 cup vanilla (***not*** plain) yogurt
1/8 cup Grape-Nuts cereal

Way to make it:

- ☐ Wash the berries (if using fresh) in your strainer and discard any stems
- ☐ Place 2 Tablespoons berries in the bottom of a custard cup
- ☐ Spoon 1/2 cup of vanilla yogurt on top of the berries
- ☐ Sprinkle 1/8 cup of Grape-Nuts cereal on top of the yogurt

Going bananas

Bananas are a tropical fruit, so don't refrigerate them. They look nice sitting in a bowl on the counter, anyway.

Buy them when they are a bit green and allow to ripen for a few days. But just because the skins turn black a week later doesn't mean they aren't edible. In fact that's the sweetest they'll ever be and a perfect time to drop them into your blender or slice them into your yogurt.

TIP: For a great sugar-free treat, pop a couple of ripe (yellow) bananas into your freezer. The skins will turn all black and look ugly. Peel off the skins and you've got nature's Popsicle.

Yo-Bananas

Makes one serving

Things you need:

Knife
Cutting board
Custard cup
Tablespoon

Food you need:

6 slices of ripe banana
1/2 cup vanilla yogurt
1/8 cup spoon-size shredded wheat cereal*

Way to make it:

- ☐ Slice banana into 6 coin-shaped rounds
- ☐ Place banana slices on bottom of a custard cup
- ☐ Cover the banana with 1/2 cup vanilla yogurt using a Tablespoon as a scoop
- ☐ Top the yogurt with 1/8 cup shredded wheat

*** Actual conversation:**

Can you use any other kind of cereal?—Ed.

No. Just shredded wheat.—Auth.

Why? What's the difference.—Ed.

There's a difference.—Auth.

What's the difference?—Ed.

There's a difference.—Auth.

Editor's note (made after the Author has seen the above): Use whatever cereal you want.

Going Ethnic

eating excitement without the energy

Avocado info

This exotic fruit is loaded with vitamin C, but also packs a high fat content. Who cares, it tastes great! Depending on type and origin, avocados come in various sizes. For guacamole *(look over yonder☞)*, the large, heavy variety is fine, but if you want a treat for yourself, go for the petite Haydens or Haas — they'll be labeled at the market. Then slice it up and sprinkle with a little lemon juice. Awwwesome!

The fruit should be soft to the touch when it's ripe. Usually the skin will turn black as a reminder that it's ready to eat. It's a good idea to buy avocados a few days before you're ready to use them and allow them to ripen at room temperature until soft.*

TIP: If you can't find a ripe one, and the party is tonight, you can soften one in the microwave. Just prick it with a knife in two or three places to prevent explosion and microcook on HIGH for 30 seconds. This will not turn the skin black, but will soften it up enough to use in the recipe.

Make sure you toss the cut avocado well with lemon or lime juice as soon as you cut it, because it will discolor rapidly. Then keep it covered in a glass or plastic container and refrigerate.

THE RECIPES

*** One friend of mine did rub suntan oil on them and stick them in little lawn chairs in the sun for a few hours, but he met with limited success.—Auth.**

Uh, your friend . . . his name didn't happen to be Elvis, did it?—Ed.

Guacamole Olé

Makes 1-1/2 cups

Things you need:

Knife
Cutting board
Mixing spoon
Blender
Tablespoon
Teaspoon
1-cup measure
1-quart bowl
Plastic wrap

Food you need:

1 large ripe avocado
2 scallions, cut into 1-inch pieces
1 Tablespoon lime ***or*** lemon juice (fresh ***or*** bottled)
1/4 teaspoon garlic powder
1/2 teaspoon chili powder
1/8 teaspoon hot sauce
1/4 cup sour cream

Way to make it:

- ☐ Cut an avocado in half lengthwise (the long way), then twist the halves apart and remove and discard pit *(or, better yet, see the next page)*
- ☐ Cut 2 scallions into 1-inch pieces
- ☐ Put the scallion pieces into your blender and chop into little pieces by pushing the **"pulse"** button or toggle switch about 6 times
- ☐ With a spoon, scoop avocado into blender and discard the skin
- ☐ Add 1 Tablespoon lime juice, 1/4 teaspoon garlic powder, 1/2 teaspoon chili powder, and 1/8 teaspoon hot sauce to blender and whirl on HIGH speed until finely chopped
- ☐ Add 1/4 cup sour cream and whirl on HIGH speed until smooth
- ☐ Place in your 1-quart bowl, cover with plastic wrap, and chill 1 hour or more

TIP: This may be frozen for up to one month in a tightly covered container.

How to grow an exotic house plant for free

Don't discard the stone (pit) from your avocado. Instead, poke three toothpicks into the pit at an imaginary center point between the stem end and the pointed end (see illustration).

This will create a tripod to support the pit in the water.

Fill a small glass with water and suspend the pit on the toothpicks, stem (round) side down, with the top elevated above the water line.

DO NOT SUBMERGE THE WHOLE PIT!

Keep the water level up and in a few weeks you'll have a full root system and at least two leaves. Now you can transplant it into a soil-filled pot.

These plants will grow as big as their container allows — up to 6 feet indoors. If you live in the tropics, plant it outside and you'll have a fruit-bearing shade tree in about 15 years.

Black Beans & Rice

Makes two servings

Things you need:

Cutting board
Knife
Tablespoon
Can opener
1-quart bowl
Teaspoon
Mixing spoon

Food you need:

1/4 chopped onion (about 1 Tablespoon) *(see page 55)*
1/4 chopped tomato (about 1 Tablespoon) *(see page 56)*
1/2 can black beans, drained *(see page 66)*
1/4 teaspoon garlic powder
1 Tablespoon butter ***or*** margarine
1 cup cooked rice *(see page 49)*

Way to make it:

- ☐ Chop 1/4 each of an onion and a tomato (this will give you about 1 Tablespoon of each)
- ☐ Drain can of black beans
- ☐ Place one Tablespoon butter ***or*** margarine, along with the onion and tomato, in your 1-quart bowl
- ☐ Add 1/4 teaspoon garlic powder
- ☐ Microcook on HIGH 1 minute
- ☐ Add 1/2 can of black beans, stir with your mixing spoon, and microcook on HIGH for 2 minutes
- ☐ Add 1 cup cooked rice, stir lightly, and microcook on HIGH another 2 minutes

Holy cheeses and others*

Cheese comes in a whole bunch of varieties.

Soft cheese such as cottage, ricotta, feta, or cream cheese can be added to the recipes in little dollops. They will quickly melt into an omelet or slither into baked ziti.

Semi-hard cheese such as Monterey Jack, Muenster, or Gouda can be used grated on top of your tacos or melted briefly in nachos, but gets gummy when really cooked.

Hard cheese is great for cooking. These cheeses include cheddar, provolone, Swiss, and super-aged Parmesan and Romano. You can substitute one for another in all the recipes . . . use what you have on hand.

Processed cheese (non-dairy American, anything that says "processed cheese food product") is just as it sounds and not very tasty, even though it is a staple in American households. It will keep in the refrigerator for what seems like years, but that is its most redeeming quality and should tell you something.

Try to experiment and use this great natural product that's a good source of protein and a very quick snack.

TIP: Store all cheese tightly wrapped in plastic and refrigerated. If a little mold grows on an edge, just cut it off — it won't hurt you (the blue in blue cheese is mold). But if it looks like a science project and starts independent movement, throw it out.

* See note on page 79. (These two just didn't get along.)

Quesadillas

Makes two quesadillas

Things you need:

Optional: Grater
Microsafe plate
1-cup measure

Food you need:

1/2 cup grated cheese (cheddar or Monterey Jack, packaged ***or*** see page 52)
2 flour tortillas
Optional: Other fillings such as salsa, sliced onions, chopped tomatoes, chopped chilies, refried beans

Way to make it:

- ☐ ***Optional:*** Grate 1/2 cup of cheese, using coarse side of grater or slicing side ***or*** open a package of pre-grated
- ☐ With your hand, spread 1/4 cup of cheese over half of each tortilla
- ☐ ***Optional:*** If you want to add some more excitement, add a small amount of other fillings (1 Tablespoonful to 1/4 cup) on top of the cheese
- ☐ Fold other half of tortilla on top of fillings and cheese
- ☐ Place on microsafe plate and put in microwave oven
- ☐ Microcook on HIGH for 1 minute, or until cheese melts
- ☐ Eat right away

Taco Smells

Makes 4 tacos

Things you need:

Cutting board
Knife
1-quart bowl
Teaspoon
Mixing spoon
Optional: Grater
1-cup measure
9-inch microsafe pie plate
Tablespoon

Food you need:

1/2 small onion, chopped *(see page 55)*
1/2 pound ground beef
1 teaspoon chili powder
1/4 teaspoon garlic powder
1/4 teaspoon seasoned salt
1/8 teaspoon hot sauce
4 taco shells
1/2 cup grated cheddar cheese *(packaged* ***or*** *see page 52)*
A bottle of salsa

Optional garnishes:
shredded lettuce *(see page 94)*
chopped tomatoes }
chopped scallions } *(see pages 55 & 56)*

Way to make it:

- ☐ Chop 1/2 onion
- ☐ Crumble 1/2 pound beef into bowl
- ☐ Add 1 teaspoon chili powder, 1/4 teaspoon garlic powder, 1/4 teaspoon seasoned salt, and 1/8 teaspoon hot sauce
- ☐ Mix well with mixing spoon
- ☐ Microcook on HIGH for 3-1/2 minutes
- ☐ ***Optional:*** Grate the cheese while this is cooking to make 1/2 cup
- ☐ Remove beef mixture from microwave and stir well
- ☐ Microcook on HIGH an additional 2 minutes
- ☐ Drain off fat from bowl into sink
- ☐ Put 4 taco shells on the pie plate
- ☐ Divide meat mixture into shells
- ☐ Sprinkle with cheese and top with salsa

Spicy Stuffed Peppers

Makes one serving

Things you need:

Knife
Cutting board
Tablespoon
Teaspoon
Optional: Grater
Microsafe plate

Food you need:

One 4-ounce can whole green chilies
3 Tablespoons cream cheese
3 Tablespoons grated cheddar ***or*** Monterey Jack cheese (packaged ***or*** fresh, *see page 52)*
3 Tablespoons bottled salsa

Way to make it:

- ☐ Drain the can of chile peppers and slit one side lengthwise *(just cut one side, don't cut into two pieces)*
- ☐ Place peppers on a flat plate
- ☐ Put 1 teaspoon of grated cheddar ***or*** Monterey Jack ***and*** cream cheese inside each pepper
- ☐ Close up peppers and top each with 1 teaspoon of salsa
- ☐ Microcook on HIGH for 1 minute

Chilly Chicken

Makes two servings

Things you need:

Knife
Cutting board
Teaspoon
Tablespoon
1-cup measure
2-1/2-quart bowl
Mixing spoon
Plastic wrap

Food you need:

Cooking spray
1 boneless, skinless chicken breast, cut in 1-inch cubes
1 small onion, chopped
1 green pepper, chopped } *(see page 55)*
1 tomato, chopped *(see page 56)*
1/2 teaspoon garlic powder
1/8 teaspoon hot sauce
1 Tablespoon Worcestershire sauce
2 Tablespoons vinegar
1 cup bottled chili sauce (located near the ketchup)
1 cup canned black beans, drained *(see page 66)*

Way to make it:

- ☐ Spray 2-1/2-quart bowl with cooking spray
- ☐ Cut chicken breast in 1-inch cubes
- ☐ Chop one small onion, 1 green pepper, and 1 small tomato into 1-inch cubes
- ☐ Using your mixing spoon, combine the chicken, onion, pepper, 1/2 teaspoon garlic powder, 1/8 teaspoon hot sauce, and 1 Tablespoon Worcestershire sauce in your 2-1/2-quart bowl
- ☐ Cover with plastic wrap and microcook on HIGH 6 minutes
- ☐ Stir 1 chopped tomato, 2 Tablespoons vinegar, and 1 cup bottled chili sauce into chicken mixture
- ☐ Drain 1 cup black beans and add to chicken
- ☐ Cover again and microcook on HIGH 10 minutes

Sweet & Sour Pork (or Chicken)

Makes two servings

Things you need:

Knife	1-quart bowl	Teaspoon	Can opener
Cutting board	Tablespoon	Mixing spoon	Plastic wrap

Food you need:

1/2 pound cubed pork **or** chicken *(buy any kind of boneless pork and prepare the same as chicken — see page 70)*
1 Tablespoon cornstarch
1/2 small onion, peeled and cut in wedges
1/2 green pepper, cut in wedges
1 Tablespoon soy sauce
1 Tablespoon sugar
2 Tablespoons vinegar
1/8 teaspoon ginger
1 cup pineapple chunks, with the juice
2 cups cooked rice *(see page 49)*

Way to make it:

- ☐ Cut 1/2 pound pork into 1-inch cubes
- ☐ Put meat in 1-quart bowl, add 1 Tablespoon cornstarch, and toss to coat
- ☐ Cut 1/2 small onion into wedges
- ☐ Cut 1/2 green pepper into wedges and remove the stem and seeds
- ☐ To the pork mixture, add 1 Tablespoon soy sauce, 1 Tablespoon sugar, 2 Tablespoons vinegar, 1/8 teaspoon ginger, and 1 cup of pineapple chunks along with the juice, onion wedges, and pepper pieces
- ☐ Stir, cover with plastic wrap, and microcook on HIGH for 10 minutes
- ☐ Let stand 5 minutes before serving with rice

** Great recipe. I need some good Chinese food.—Ed.*

What happened to, what's his name?—Auth.

Dennis? Old story. There's this guy over at Wings 'n' Things. . . . —Ed.

Oh nooo, spare me, please! Look, turn the page. Make some wings. Take a cold shower. — Auth.

Buying chicken wings

A natural chicken wing has three sections: the shoulder-to-elbow part has one big bone, just like your arm; the elbow-to-wrist part has 2 bones; and the tip, which has about as much meat on it as your hand does.

If you buy whole chicken wings you are going to be spending a lot of time separating each wing into three sections and then throwing all the tips away. You don't need to be in the MBA program to figure out that this is not cost-effective.

Most markets offer butchered wings in either fresh or frozen packages. These are sometimes marketed as "Drummettes." The frozen are especially cheap and convenient. They are individually frozen so you can pull out only as many as you need, reseal the package, and pop it back in the freezer. Just follow the directions on the box to defrost.

Wings en Fuego

Makes 12 pieces

Things you need:

4 paper towels
9-inch microsafe pie plate
Knife
Cutting board
Fork

Food you need:

12 frozen chicken wing sections, defrosted *(great info over there ☜)*
1 Tablespoon cornstarch
1 Tablespoon hot sauce, then . . .
1 teaspoon hot sauce
Bottle of blue cheese dressing
4 ribs celery *(see page 86)*

Way to make it:

- ☐ Pat the 12 defrosted chicken wings dry with paper towels
- ☐ Place wings in pie plate, dust with 1 Tablespoon cornstarch
- ☐ Sprinkle wings with 1 Tablespoon hot sauce
- ☐ Arrange the wings on the plate like the spokes of a wheel *(see next page)*
- ☐ Microcook on HIGH for 8 minutes
- ☐ Wash celery and slice each rib lengthwise in 2 pieces, then cut in half crosswise to get 4 pieces, total
- ☐ Using your fork, turn the wings over and microcook on HIGH 4 minutes longer
- ☐ Remove from microwave
- ☐ Sprinkle 1 teaspoon of hot sauce over the wings
- ☐ Serve with blue cheese and celery sticks

HINT: If you like "wings on fire," just add more hot sauce.

How to arrange wings on the pie plate*

* "One picture is worth more than ten thousand words." Ancient Chinese proverb. — Auth.

"One bad egg roll is worth 10,000 prunes." Ancient Chinese delivery boyfriend.— Ed.

You know, you should be locked up someplace far, far away from civilized humanity.— Auth.

Kung Fu Wings

Makes 12 chicken wings

Things you need:

3 paper towels
1-quart bowl
Mixing spoon
Tablespoon
Teaspoon
9-inch microsafe pie plate
Fork

Food you need:

12 frozen chicken wing sections, defrosted *(see page 144)*
1 Tablespoon soy sauce
1/4 teaspoon sugar
1/2 teaspoon ginger
1 teaspoon cinnamon
1 Tablespoon cornstarch
1 Tablespoon water

Way to make it:

- ☐ Pat chicken dry with paper towels
- ☐ Mix all ingredients — except chicken — in your 1-quart bowl
- ☐ With your mixing spoon, toss the chicken in this marinade and let it sit for 15 minutes
- ☐ Place chicken like the spokes of a wheel on a glass pie plate *(cast your eyes left ☜)*
- ☐ Microcook on HIGH for 10 minutes
- ☐ Turn chicken pieces over with your fork
- ☐ Microcook on HIGH for an additional 4 minutes
- ☐ Serve warm or cold

Picadillo

In Spanish, ***picadillo*** means little snack.* This robust dish is hardly a snack, more like a feast.

But with the great hospitality I've been shown by my South American buddies, I can see where the distinction blurs. There is always so much food, friends, and family around and the tables groan with meats, fish, pastries, and the like that — at least in the Yanez family — this would in fact qualify as a snack.

*This **very** savory dish is worth the effort.*

THE RECIPES

* *Actually,* picadillo *is minced meat, or minced meat and vegetables. Perhaps you are mistaking it for* bocadillo *or* panecillo salado, *which is a cocktail snack.— Ed.*

Perhaps you are mistaking my fist, which is New York for a knuckle sandwich!— Auth.

Picadillo

Makes two servings

Things you need:

Cutting board
Knife
1-quart bowl
Plastic wrap
Soup bowl
Fork
1-cup measure
Teaspoon
Tablespoon

Food you need:

1/2 medium onion, chopped *(see page 55)*
1/2 green pepper, seeded and chopped *(also on 55)*
1/4 teaspoon garlic powder
Cooking spray
1/2 pound ground beef
1/8 cup ketchup
1 Tablespoon sugar
1/4 teaspoon curry powder
1/4 teaspoon salt
1/4 teaspoon pepper
1/8 teaspoon cinnamon
1/4 cup raisins
1/4 cup stuffed green olives, drained *(see page 98)*

Way to make it:

- ☐ Chop 1/2 medium onion and 1/2 green pepper
- ☐ Spray 1-quart bowl with cooking spray
- ☐ To your 1-quart bowl, add the chopped onion, chopped peppers, and 1/4 teaspoon garlic powder
- ☐ Cover with plastic wrap and microcook on HIGH for 2 minutes
- ☐ Crumble beef into bowl and stir into onion/pepper mixture
- ☐ Re-cover with plastic wrap, cook on HIGH for 2 minutes
- ☐ In a soup bowl, stir together with a fork: 1/8 cup ketchup, 1 Tablespoon sugar, 1/4 teaspoon curry powder, 1/4 teaspoon salt, 1/4 teaspoon pepper, 1/8 teaspoon cinnamon
- ☐ Stir into beef mixture, breaking up any lumps of meat
- ☐ Cover with plastic wrap and microcook on HIGH for 3 minutes
- ☐ Add 1/4 cup raisins and 1/4 cup olives (drained)
- ☐ Microcook on HIGH for 3 minutes

TIP: This is GREAT served with rice and beans *(see page 137)* for a hearty meal.

Phat Meatballs

Makes 15 little meatballs

Things you need:

Tablespoon
Teaspoon
1-quart bowl
Glass pie plate
Paper towel
Toothpicks

Food you need:

1/2 pound ground beef
2 Tablespoons bread crumbs
2 Tablespoons soy sauce
1 teaspoon sugar
1/2 teaspoon ground ginger
Cooking spray

Way to make it:

- ☐ Wash your hands*
- ☐ With your hands, mix 1/2 pound ground beef, 2 Tablespoons bread crumbs, 2 Tablespoons soy sauce, 1 teaspoon sugar, and 1/2 teaspoon ground ginger in a 1-quart bowl
- ☐ Spray glass pie plate with cooking spray
- ☐ Shape meat mixture into 1-inch round balls
- ☐ Place meatballs evenly around pie plate
- ☐ Cover with paper towel
- ☐ Microcook on HIGH for 6 minutes
- ☐ Serve with toothpicks as a snack or over pasta for dinner

TIP: This magic recipe makes its own sauce!

*** You always do this, right?—Auth.**
Oh yeah, right.—Ed.

Cheater's Pad Thai

Makes two servings

Things you need:

1-quart measuring pitcher
2-1/2-quart bowl
Mixing spoon
1-cup measure
Tablespoon
Teaspoon
Cutting board
Knife
Fork
Plastic wrap

Food you need:

3 cups water
1/4 pound thin spaghetti
1/8 cup chicken broth (canned ***or*** bouillon cubes or granules — *see page 19*)
2 Tablespoons Thai fish sauce (available in oriental markets ***or*** substitute soy sauce)
1/2 teaspoon garlic powder
1/4 pound ground pork ***or*** turkey (you can get it from the supermarket)
1 scallion, chopped *(see page 55)*
1/4 pound precooked and shelled shrimp, defrosted if frozen
1 egg, beaten with a fork
1 Tablespoon lemon juice (fresh ***or*** bottled)
1/2 cup bean sprouts (fresh ***or*** canned)
1 Tablespoon peanuts

Way to make it:

- ☐ Add 3 cups water to 1-quart measuring pitcher and microcook on HIGH for 5 minutes
- ☐ Add 1/4 pound thin spaghetti, broken in half, to water. Microcook on HIGH for 5 minutes. Drain

(continued)

- ☐ In a 2-1/2-quart bowl, use your mixing spoon to combine 1/8 cup chicken broth, 2 Tablespoons fish sauce, and 1/2 teaspoon garlic powder
- ☐ Crumble in 1/4 pound ground pork (***or*** turkey)
- ☐ Microcook on HIGH for 5 minutes
- ☐ Chop scallion
- ☐ Slice shrimp in half lengthwise (the long way)
- ☐ Beat 1 egg with a fork
- ☐ Add spaghetti and beaten egg to the meat mixture.
- ☐ Stir, cover with plastic wrap, and microcook on HIGH for 3 minutes
- ☐ Place shrimp on top of mixture and microcook on HIGH for 1 minute
- ☐ Sprinkle with lemon juice, then use your mixing spoon to toss with 1/2 cup bean sprouts, 1 chopped scallion, and 1 Tablespoon peanuts

Siam sez...

Try this dish! I have not included this recipe in the regular menu because it has a grand list of ingredients and takes careful attention to the directions. But many of my test kitchen helpers wanted a Thai dish in the book, so we tried it.*

The fish sauce is a signature flavor in Thai cooking, but if it is not available where you live, you can substitute soy sauce.

THE RECIPES

* *Showoff!—Ed.*

Japanese Noodles

Makes two servings

Things you need:

Strainer
1-cup measure
Paper towel
Cutting board
Knife
Plastic wrap
Teaspoon
Can opener
1-quart bowl

Food you need:

One handful fresh, whole-leaf, pre-washed spinach *(see page 90)*
3 cups water
About 6 ounces of angel hair pasta *(see page 47)*
1/4 pound round steak, sliced thin *(see* ***TIP*** *on the next ☞ page)*
1 carrot, sliced in coin shapes
1 medium onion, sliced
2 scallions, cut in 1-inch pieces
1/2 small (7-ounce) can mushroom stems and pieces, drained *(see page 66)*

3/4 cup chicken broth
1/8 cup soy sauce
1 teaspoon sugar
} MIXED TOGETHER

Way to make it:

- ☐ Rinse one handful of fresh, whole-leaf, pre-washed spinach in your strainer over the sink
- ☐ Put aside to drain — leave it in your strainer in the sink
- ☐ Put 3 cups of water in your measuring pitcher
- ☐ Add the 6 ounces of angel hair pasta to the water, microcook on HIGH for 5 minutes
- ☐ Put the cooked pasta in the strainer with the spinach to drain

(continued)

- [ ] Slice 1/4 pound round steak in thin strips
- [ ] Slice 1 carrot in coin-shaped rounds
- [ ] Cut 2 scallions in 1-inch pieces
- [ ] Cut 1 small onion into eight pieces (first into 4 wedges, then cut each wedge in half through the middle)*
- [ ] Mix 3/4 cup chicken broth, 1/8 cup soy sauce, and 1 teaspoon sugar in your 1-quart bowl
- [ ] Add carrots, onions, scallions, and ***half*** the can of mushrooms to your bowl
- [ ] Microcook on HIGH for 2 minutes
- [ ] Add the noodles, the spinach, and the beef
- [ ] Cover with plastic wrap and microcook on HIGH for 6 minutes

TIP: The steak will cut easier if it is partially frozen, or at least cold, when you slice it.

THE RECIPES

* *Hey, I thought you said these recipes would be easy to make!—Ed.*

OK, I know I said no complicated recipes in this book. But this is one yummy dish, and you can try it on a vacation day or feed it to your soul mate with Japanese tea. Just sit on the floor and dream of the Orient!—Auth.

Chicken Chow Mein

Serves one fullback or 3 ballet majors
(and cooks easier than it reads!)

Things you need:

1-cup measure
1-quart measuring pitcher
Cutting board
Knife
1-quart bowl
Tablespoon
Teaspoon
Vegetable peeler
Plastic wrap
Can opener
Mixing spoon
Fork

Food you need:

1 cup rice
2 cups water
1 boneless chicken breast cut in bite-sized pieces **or** 6 chicken tenderloins *(see **HINT** way over on the next ☞ page)*
1/2 Tablespoon soy sauce, then . . .
2 Tablespoons soy sauce, then . . .
1 Tablespoon soy sauce
1/8 teaspoon ground ginger
1 rib celery *(see page 86)*
1 carrot
1/4 cup canned mushroom stems and pieces (drained)
1/4 cup water chestnuts (drained)
1/2 cup canned bean sprouts (drained)
} *(see page 66)*
1/2 cup chicken broth
1 Tablespoon water
1 teaspoon cornstarch
1 can ***or*** package of chow mein noodles (found in ethnic section at your market)

(continued)

Way to make it:

- ☐ Place 1 cup of rice and 2 cups of water in your 1-quart measuring pitcher
- ☐ Microcook, uncovered, on HIGH for 10 minutes
- ☐ Cut up chicken into bite-size pieces
- ☐ Place uncooked chicken in your 1-quart bowl and mix with 1/2 Tablespoon of soy sauce and 1/8 teaspoon of ginger
- ☐ With vegetable peeler, peel carrot and slice thinly — on the diagonal is esthetically desirable*
- ☐ Slice celery thinly, on the diagonal
- ☐ Remove rice from microwave and let sit, covered with plastic wrap, until ready to serve (at least 10 minutes)
- ☐ Open canned mushrooms, water chestnuts, and bean sprouts and drain
- ☐ Add celery, carrots, and broth to the chicken in the bowl, mix with your mixing spoon
- ☐ Cover with plastic wrap and microcook on HIGH for 3 minutes
- ☐ Mix 2 Tablespoons soy sauce, 1 Tablespoon water, and 1 Tablespoon cornstarch in your 1-cup measure
- ☐ Stir into chicken and vegetables
- ☐ Cover with plastic wrap, and return to oven and microcook on HIGH for 5 minutes longer
- ☐ Add 1 Tablespoon soy sauce and stir
- ☐ Fluff rice with fork
- ☐ Serve chicken over 1 cup of rice for each serving
- ☐ Garnish with chow mein noodles

HINT: You can buy chicken tenderloins — that soft little "extra" part that's attached to a breast — individually frozen in many markets. They are cheap and convenient if you have a freezer, and may be substituted for breast in all the recipes.

* *Esthetically desirable?!—Ed.*

Woman does not live by bread alone.—Auth.

Home Cookin'

microcooking like Grandma used to do

Macaroni and cheese confessions

In spite of all efforts to educate my children in the most unusual of culinary experiences, they still always wanted the macaroni and cheese dinner that comes in the blue box. So if you retain that nostalgic link to childhood, here are some ideas to jazz up the plate, turning you into a gourmet chef of extraordinary creativity.*

Mac 'n' Cheese Du Jour

Things you need:

See next page ☞

Food you need:

A box of macaroni and cheese "dinner"

Way to make it:

- ☐ Make a macaroni and cheese dinner according to manufacturer's directions
- ☐ Add any of the following *(see page numbers for microcooking directions)*:

  Cooked chopped broccoli } *(see page 204)*
  Cooked chopped cauliflower }
  A few cooked peas
  Crumbled cooked bacon *(see page 63)*
  Cooked sliced hot dogs *(microcook them on HIGH for a minute)*
  Salsa **or** stewed tomatoes (use on top)
  Packaged seasoned bread crumbs (sprinkle on top)
  Any deli meats (slice in)

HINT: This is another great way to clean the leftovers from your fridge.

* *Barf.—Ed.*

Mac 'n' Cheese

Makes two servings

Things you need:

1-quart measure
1-cup measure
Strainer
1-quart bowl
Tablespoon
Teaspoon
Optional: Grater
Mixing spoon

Food you need:

3 cups water
1 cup elbow ***or*** small shell pasta
1 Tablespoon butter ***or*** margarine
1 Tablespoon cornstarch
1 teaspoon mustard
1/2 cup milk
1 cup shredded ***or*** grated yellow cheese (packaged American, cheddar, Monterey Jack, etc. ***or*** *see page 52*)

Way to make it:

- ☐ Put 3 cups water in the quart measure and microcook on HIGH for 7 minutes
- ☐ Add 1 cup pasta to water and microcook on HIGH for 7 minutes more
- ☐ Drain pasta in strainer over sink
- ☐ Put 1 Tablespoon butter ***or*** margarine in a 1-quart bowl and microcook on HIGH for 30 seconds
- ☐ With your Tablespoon, blend 1 Tablespoon cornstarch and 1 teaspoon mustard into butter ***or*** margarine
- ☐ Stir in 1/2 cup milk
- ☐ Microcook uncovered on HIGH for 3 minutes, then stir well with mixing spoon

The gritty truth

For those of you residing north of the Mason-Dixon line, the name of this dish can be off-putting. But grits are not gritty. In fact, they are a creamy alternative to oatmeal or creamed wheat for breakfast. You can omit the cheese shown in the recipe and simply add a little butter or margarine and some salt and pepper or maple syrup for a fine southern hot breakfast.

Grits also work well as a side dish with simply prepared meat and vegetables. The addition of mushrooms (canned, drained, stems-and-pieces work fine), chopped scallion, and a sprinkling of Parmesan cheese turn this corn grain into a Southern party dish.

Cheese Grits

Makes one serving

Things you need:

1-quart bowl
Tablespoon
1-cup measure
Mixing spoon
Grater

Food you need:

3/4 cup water
3 Tablespoons "quick" grits
1 Tablespoon cheddar cheese *(packaged **or** fresh grated, see page 52)*
Salt

Way to make it:

- ☐ Put 3 Tablespoons of "quick" grits and 3/4 cup water and a dash of salt in your 1-quart bowl
- ☐ Stir with your mixing spoon
- ☐ Microcook on HIGH for 4 minutes, until thick
- ☐ Meanwhile, open a package of grated cheddar cheese ***or*** grate 1 Tablespoon cheddar cheese
- ☐ Remove grits from oven
- ☐ Stir in 1 Tablespoon grated cheese

Potato facts

There are several types of potatoes available at the market. All the recipes in this book were tested with russet (Idaho) potatoes, but by trying different kinds in the recipes, you'll achieve different flavors and textures. Here's the list:

Russet (Idaho) potatoes are elongated with thick "barky" skins. They range in size from medium to large and make great bakers.

Boiling potatoes are round and thin skinned. They are medium-sized and come in both red and white. They are good for soups, stews, potato salad, and mashed potatoes.

New potatoes live up to their name. They are small, thin-skinned in red or white, and are wonderful steamed.

Yukon Gold are medium to large potatoes with a distinctive yellow flesh. They have a buttery taste that eliminates the need for added fat after baking.

Dinner-in-a-Jacket

Makes one serving

Things you need:

Vegetable brush
Knife
Paper towel

Food you need:

1 baking potato

Way to make it:

- ☐ Scrub potato with water using vegetable brush
- ☐ Pierce the potato in three places with your knife
- ☐ Place the potato on a piece of paper towel in your microwave
- ☐ Microcook on HIGH for 3 to 4 minutes, until soft
- ☐ Cut open lengthwise and top with any combination listed below:

TOPPERS

Grated cheese (any kind)
Salsa
Chopped scallions
Sour cream
Butter ***or*** margarine
Chili
Jalapeño peppers
Crumbled bacon
Spaghetti sauce
Cooked vegetables (use up your leftovers)

HINT: Potatoes really shouldn't be stored in the refrigerator; they tend to take on various smells and the starch turns to sugar.*

THE RECIPES

** Yeah, right. Where do you keep your potatoes?—Ed.*

Well, in the refrigerator. But they really should be kept in a cool, dark place. And at least don't put onions in the same container.—Auth.

Porsche Potatoes

Makes two servings

Things you need:

Glass pie plate
3 pieces paper towel
Knife
Cutting board
Tablespoon
Teaspoon
1-cup measure
1-quart bowl
Potholders

Food you need:

2 strips of bacon (pork, turkey, ***or*** vegetarian)
1 large potato
1 Tablespoon sugar
1/2 Tablespoon cornstarch
1/2 teaspoon seasoned salt
1/4 teaspoon mustard
1/4 cup water
1/4 cup vinegar
1 scallion, chopped *(see page 55)*

Way to make it:

- ☐ Put 2 strips of bacon on a paper towel in your pie plate and microcook on HIGH for 3 minutes
- ☐ Remove bacon on towel and let cool
- ☐ Wash potato and pierce with the tip of a knife in 3 places
- ☐ Put in microwave on a piece of paper towel and microcook on HIGH for 4 minutes, until soft
- ☐ Remove potato from oven and let cool
- ☐ In a 1-quart bowl, put 1 Tablespoon sugar, 1/2 Tablespoon cornstarch, 1/2 teaspoon seasoned salt, 1/4 teaspoon mustard, 1/4 cup water, 1/4 cup vinegar, and 1 chopped scallion and stir together with your mixing spoon
- ☐ Microcook the mixture on HIGH for 2 minutes
- ☐ Cut the potato into 1/4-inch thick slices. Toss into sauce
- ☐ Crumble bacon and add to potato mixture and microcook on HIGH for 2 more minutes

Buddha's Private Idaho

Makes two servings

Things you need:

Strainer
1-quart bowl
1-cup measure
Vegetable brush
Cutting board
Knife
Teaspoon
Tablespoon
Plastic wrap

Food you need:

Cooking spray
1-cup mixed fresh **or** frozen vegetables (whatever you have), defrosted and drained
1 cup cubed potatoes (no need to peel) *(see page 55)*
1/2 cup water
1 vegetable bouillon cube **or** 1 teaspoon granules *(see page 19)**
1/4 medium onion, chopped *(see page 55)*
1/4 teaspoon garlic powder
Salt and pepper to taste

Way to make it:

- ☐ Defrost and drain 1-cup of mixed vegetables in your strainer in the sink
- ☐ Spray 1-quart bowl with cooking spray
- ☐ Wash one potato and cut into 1-inch cubes — you do *not* need to peel them
- ☐ With your Tablespoon, mix potato, 1/2 cup water, 1/4 teaspoon garlic powder, and bouillon in the bowl
- ☐ Cover with plastic wrap, microcook 3 minutes on HIGH
- ☐ Add 1 cup mixed vegetables and 1/4 medium onion, chopped
- ☐ Microcook on HIGH for 3 minutes
- ☐ Add salt and pepper to taste

* ***REMEMBER:*** *Knorr* vegetable bouillon makes 2 cups, so use only 1/2 cube in recipes calling for 1 cup of water.

Smashed Potatoes

Makes two servings

Things you need:

Paper towel
Knife
Tablespoon
1-quart bowl
Fork

Food you need:

2 large potatoes
1/2 cup milk
3 Tablespoons butter ***or*** margarine
Salt and pepper to taste

Way to make it:

- ☐ Place 2 potatoes on a paper towel on the oven floor
- ☐ Microcook on HIGH for 8 minutes
- ☐ Remove from oven and allow to cool until they can be easily handled
- ☐ Slice potatoes in half horizontally (the long way)
- ☐ With a Tablespoon, remove the flesh from the potatoes and place in your 1-quart bowl
- ☐ Mash with a fork until well crumbled
- ☐ With your Tablespoon, stir in 1/2 cup milk and 3 Tablespoons butter ***or*** margarine
- ☐ Season with salt and pepper
- ☐ Return to microwave and heat on HIGH for 1 minute, until hot

HINT: For another meal, save the potato skins, top with your favorite topper *(see page 163)*, and microcook on HIGH for 1 minute.

Barbecued Chicken Wings

Makes 12 wings

Things you need:

Glass pie plate
1-cup measure

Food you need:

12 chicken wings
1/4 cup barbecue sauce (buy your favorite)

Way to make it:

- ☐ Place wings like spokes of a wheel on a glass pie plate *(see below)*
- ☐ Microcook on HIGH for 8 minutes
- ☐ Pour sauce on top and turn to coat well
- ☐ Microcook on HIGH for 1 minute to warm sauce

Hot Dogs Hungary*

Makes enough for two,
or one really hungry guy

Things you need:

1-quart bowl
Knife
1-cup measure
Plastic wrap
Cutting board
Teaspoon
Can opener
Mixing spoon

Food you need:

Cooking spray
1 green pepper, seeded and chopped into 1-inch cubes } *(see page 55)*
1 medium onion, coarsely chopped } *(see page 55)*
1/4 teaspoon garlic powder
1 cup canned diced *(already diced,* ***or*** *see page 56)* tomatoes, undrained
1/4 teaspoon salt
1/8 teaspoon pepper
2 teaspoons paprika
2 hot dogs cut in 1-inch pieces
1 cup dry broad egg noodles, then cook as in recipe for Single Serving Pasta *(see page 47)*

Way to make it:

- ☐ Spray a 1-quart microsafe casserole with cooking spray
- ☐ Cut onion and green pepper into 1-inch cubes
- ☐ Place onion, 1/4 teaspoon garlic, and peppers in dish
- ☐ Microcook, uncovered, on HIGH for 3 minutes
- ☐ Add 1 cup diced tomatoes, undrained, salt, pepper, and paprika
- ☐ Microcook on HIGH for 5 minutes
- ☐ Cut hot dogs into 1-inch pieces
- ☐ Add hot dogs to vegetables in the bowl, cover with plastic wrap, and microcook on HIGH for 2 minutes
- ☐ Allow to sit for 5 minutes
- ☐ Cook noodles as in recipe for Single Serving Pasta on page 47
- ☐ Drain
- ☐ Add to casserole, stir with mixing spoon, and serve

* *This is not a misteak.—Ed.*

Creamy Ziti Bake

Makes two servings

Things you need:

1-quart measuring pitcher	***Optional:*** Grater	Teaspoon
Cutting board	Strainer	Tablespoon
Knife	1-quart bowl	Mixing spoon

Food you need:

3 cups water
1 scallion, chopped *(see page 55)*
2 Tablespoons packaged ***or*** fresh *(see page 52)* grated cheddar cheese
1 cup ziti pasta
1/4 pound chopped beef
1/2 cup canned tomato sauce
1/8 teaspoon Italian seasoning
1/8 teaspoon garlic powder
3 Tablespoons cream cheese

Way to make it:

- ☐ Put 3 cups of water in your measuring pitcher and microcook on HIGH for 5 minutes
- ☐ Chop scallions and open the cheddar cheese package ***or*** shred the cheddar cheese while waiting
- ☐ Add ziti pasta to hot water in pitcher
- ☐ Microcook on HIGH for 7 minutes
- ☐ Drain pasta in strainer over sink and set aside
- ☐ Crumble meat in 1-quart bowl. Microcook on HIGH for 2 minutes
- ☐ Add tomato sauce, Italian seasoning, garlic, and scallions and stir into meat with the mixing spoon
- ☐ With the teaspoon, drop the cream cheese in small dabs on top of the tomato mixture but . . . *DO NOT STIR IN!*
- ☐ Top with ziti pasta
- ☐ Sprinkle with cheddar cheese
- ☐ Microcook on HIGH for 5 minutes

Sloppy Joans

Makes two servings

Things you need:

Cutting board
Knife
1-quart bowl
Teaspoon
Can opener
Plastic wrap

Food you need:

2 Tablespoons chopped onion *(start with 1-inch chunks and see page 55)*
1/2 pound ground beef ***or*** turkey
1 teaspoon chili powder
1/2 teaspoon sugar
1/2 cup canned tomato sauce
Hamburger buns

Way to make it:

- ☐ Chop onion to make 2 Tablespoons
- ☐ Crumble 1/2 pound chopped meat into 1-quart bowl
- ☐ Add chopped onion to bowl
- ☐ Microcook on HIGH for 5 minutes
- ☐ Pour off liquid
- ☐ Add to bowl 1 teaspoon chili powder, 1/2 teaspoon sugar, and 1/2 cup canned tomato sauce
- ☐ Cover with plastic wrap and microcook on HIGH for 5 minutes
- ☐ Stir with teaspoon and let stand 5 minutes
- ☐ Serve on sliced hamburger buns

Chicken 'n' Dumplin's

Makes two servings

Things you need:

1-quart bowl
1-cup measure
Tablespoon
Mixing spoon
Teaspoon
Plastic wrap
Cutting board
Knife

Food you need:

3/4 cup frozen mixed vegetables (about a 1/4 package)
2 Tablespoons butter ***or*** margarine
1/8 teaspoon **each** salt and pepper
1 chicken breast, cooked and cubed *(see page 71)*
2 Tablespoons cornstarch
2/3 cup chicken broth
1/3 cup milk
1/2 cup packaged biscuit mix (like Bisquick)
2 Tablespoons milk

Way to make it:

- ☐ In your 1-quart bowl, mix 3/4 cup mixed vegetables and 2 Tablespoons butter ***or*** margarine with your mixing spoon
- ☐ Season with 1/8 teaspoon salt and 1/8 teaspoon pepper
- ☐ Cover the bowl with plastic wrap and microcook the vegetable mixture on HIGH for 3 minutes
- ☐ Cut the chicken breast into cubes
- ☐ In your 1-cup measure, add 2 Tablespoons cornstarch, 2/3 cup chicken broth, and 1/3 cup milk
- ☐ Stir well with your mixing spoon to combine and add to the vegetable mixture
- ☐ Cover and microcook on HIGH for 4 minutes; stir after 2 minutes
- ☐ Meanwhile, in your 1-cup measure, mix 1/2 cup biscuit mix and 2 Tablespoons milk and blend thoroughly with your mixing spoon
- ☐ Add the cooked and cubed chicken breast to vegetable mixture
- ☐ Place four mounds of the biscuit mix ***ON TOP OF*** the chicken and vegetables
- ☐ Microcook on HIGH, uncovered, for 5 minutes

Lemony Chicken

Makes one serving

Things you need:

Cutting board
Knife
Serving plate
Custard cup
Tablespoon
Teaspoon
Paper towel

Food you need:

1 skinless, boneless precooked chicken breast *(see page 71)*
2 onion slices
1 Tablespoon soy sauce
1 Tablespoon lemon juice (bottled ***or*** fresh)
1/4 teaspoon garlic powder

Way to make it:

- ☐ Slice 2 rounds of onion 1/4-inch thick
- ☐ Place chicken breast on a serving plate
- ☐ Scatter onion rings over chicken
- ☐ In a custard cup, use a Tablespoon to combine 1 Tablespoon soy sauce, 1 Tablespoon lemon juice, and 1/4 teaspoon garlic powder
- ☐ Pour lemon mixture over chicken
- ☐ Cover chicken lightly with paper towel and microcook on HIGH for 4 minutes

2-3?

Beef Stew

Makes two servings

Things you need:

2-1/2-quart bowl
Can opener
Teaspoon
Mixing spoon
Plastic wrap
Vegetable peeler
Cutting board
Knife

Food you need:

1/2 pound stew beef (comes already cut into cubes)
1 Tablespoon cornstarch
One 5.5-ounce can V-8 ***or*** tomato juice
One 5.5-ounce can water
1 beef bouillon cube ***or*** 1 teaspoon granules *(see page 19)*
1/4 teaspoon garlic powder
1/8 teaspoon pepper
1 raw potato, cubed in 1-inch pieces
2 carrots, sliced in 1-inch pieces
1 onion, cut in eighths
} *(see pages 54 & 55)*

Way to make it:

- ☐ In your 2-1/2-quart bowl, roll around 1/2 pound of beef in 1 Tablespoon cornstarch to coat lightly
- ☐ To the bowl, mix in beef, 1 can of V-8 ***or*** tomato juice, 1 can of water, 1 bouillon cube ***or*** 1 teaspoon granules, 1/4 teaspoon garlic powder, and 1/4 teaspoon pepper
- ☐ Cover with plastic wrap and microcook on HIGH for 5 minutes
- ☐ **Meanwhile**, get your vegetable peeler and . . .
- ☐ Peel and cut 1 potato into 1-inch cubes
- ☐ Peel and cut 2 carrots into 1-inch pieces
- ☐ Peel and cut onion into eight pieces
- ☐ Remove bowl from microwave, stir, cover with plastic wrap, and microcook on HIGH for 5 more minutes
- ☐ Add potato, carrots, and onion to bowl
- ☐ Microcook, uncovered, on HIGH for 15 minutes

Meat loaf, again . . .?

Yes, we all remember Mom stretching her food dollars with a savory meat loaf, the all-American favorite. Everyone has their preferred recipe and it's curiously always the same as Mom (Dad) made. You can add your own special ingredients to this recipe — carrots, hard-cooked eggs, oatmeal, or chicken livers. Give a call to Mom for *her* special touch and surprise her with this easy, quick variation of her most commonly cooked meal.

Meat loaf again, again...

OK, I admit it. I hate meat loaf (my Mom's was a bit less than special), but I love meat loaf sandwiches! So, I make it for the family and can't wait until tomorrow to slice it on fresh bread with lettuce and salsa and green pepper rounds. Some folks have it cold or hot (fried like a hamburger) on a roll with ketchup, mustard, BBQ sauce, or mayo. You can also add capers, olives, almost anything but peanut butter.*

Pass the pâté *s'il vous plait*

The expensive pâté you buy (well, *somebody* must buy it!) in a tiny jar is meat loaf! Just very finely chopped meat loaf. The real expensive stuff is made with goose livers — pâté foi gras. So try your recipe cold on crackers with chopped hard-cooked egg, chopped onions, some capers, and a dash of Dijon mustard as a very classy first course or snack.

THE RECIPES

** Just a . . .—Ed.*

DON'T say it!—Auth.

Meat Loaf

Makes three servings

Things you need:

Cutting board
Knife
1-quart bowl
Teaspoon
Tablespoon
Mixing spoon

Food you need:

2 Tablespoons chopped green pepper
1/3 medium onion, chopped } *(see page 55)*
1 slice any kind of bread, crumbled
1/4 teaspoon Italian seasoning
1/4 teaspoon garlic powder
1 raw egg
1 pound ground beef
1/2 cup salsa

Way to make it:

- ☐ Finely chop 2 Tablespoons green pepper
- ☐ Chop 1/3 of a medium-size onion
- ☐ Crumble 1 slice of any kind of bread into a 1-quart bowl
- ☐ Add the peppers, onion, 1/4 teaspoon Italian seasoning, and 1/4 teaspoon garlic powder to the bowl
- ☐ Break the egg and stir well into the mixture with your mixing spoon
- ☐ Add 1 pound of ground beef to the bowl and mix thoroughly
- ☐ Pat down tightly and top with 1/2 cup salsa
- ☐ Microcook on HIGH for 5 minutes.
- ☐ Carefully drain off excess liquid into sink
- ☐ Microcook on HIGH for 5 minutes more

TIP: You might want to serve topped with a ribbon of ketchup or canned gravy, or sprinkled with Parmesan cheese.

Black-Eyed Susie

Makes four servings

Things you need:

Can opener
Cutting board
Knife
1-quart bowl
Plastic wrap
A cup

Food you need:

One 15-ounce can of black-eyed peas, drained *(see page 66)*, but saving the liquid
1/2 rib celery *(see page 86)*
1/4 medium onion, chopped *(see page 55)*
1/8 pound (let's say 2 ounces) deli-sliced (***or*** packaged) smoked ham ***or*** cooked bacon
1/8 teaspoon hot sauce

Way to make it:

- ☐ Carefully pour the liquid out of a can of black-eyed peas, saving the liquid from the can in a cup
- ☐ Chop 1/2 rib of celery into 1/4-inch pieces
- ☐ Chop 1/4 of medium onion into 1/4-inch pieces
- ☐ Put the chopped celery, chopped onion, and the reserved canning liquid from the peas into a 1-quart bowl
- ☐ Add the ham
- ☐ Cover the bowl with plastic wrap and microcook on HIGH for 5 minutes
- ☐ Add the drained black-eyed peas and 1/8 teaspoon hot sauce
- ☐ Microcook on HIGH for 5 minutes

Mermaid Medley

Makes three servings

Things you need:

1-quart bowl
1-cup measure
Can opener
Teaspoon
Mixing spoon

Food you need:

2 cups frozen mixed vegetables of your choice
One 10-3/4-ounce can condensed cream of mushroom soup
1/8 teaspoon hot sauce
One 7-ounce can water-packed tuna, drained *(see page 66)*
1 cup of packaged chow mein noodles

Way to make it:

- ☐ In your 1-quart bowl, add 2 cups of frozen mixed vegetables, one 10-3/4-ounce can condensed mushroom soup — *undiluted* — and the hot sauce
- ☐ Stir with your mixing spoon until combined
- ☐ Cover with plastic wrap and microcook on HIGH for 5 minutes
- ☐ Meanwhile, open the can of tuna, drain, and discard water
- ☐ Flake into vegetable mixture and stir
- ☐ Microcook, uncovered, on HIGH for 3 minutes
- ☐ Top with packaged chow mein noodles

Veggie Stew

Makes one serving

Things you need:

Cutting board
Knife
1-quart bowl
Teaspoon
Mixing spoon
Plastic wrap

Food you need:

1/2 zucchini
1/2 summer (yellow) squash*
1/4 onion, coarsely chopped
1 small tomato, coarsely chopped } *(see pages 55 & 56)*
1/2 teaspoon garlic powder
1/2 teaspoon seasoned salt
1/8 cup water

Way to make it:

- ☐ Slice 1/2 zucchini and 1/2 summer squash into 1/4-inch slices
- ☐ Coarsely chop 1/4 onion and small tomato
- ☐ Place the vegetables in a 1-quart bowl
- ☐ Add 1/2 teaspoon garlic powder and 1/2 teaspoon seasoned salt
- ☐ Stir in 1/8 cup water with your mixing spoon
- ☐ Cover with plastic wrap and microcook on HIGH for 5 minutes

* *What if it's winter?—Ed.*
Use a winter squash.—Auth.
What if it's autumn?—Ed.
Use a salami!—Auth.

Fire Drill Chili

Makes two servings

Things you need:

Cutting board
Knife
2-1/2-quart bowl
Mixing spoon
Tablespoon
Can opener

Food you need:

1 small onion, chopped *(see page 55)*
Cooking spray
1/2 pound ground beef
2 Tablespoons chili powder
One 14-1/2-ounce can of peeled plum tomatoes, chopped
One 16-ounce can red kidney beans (drained) } *(see page 66)*
One 7-ounce can chopped green chilies (drained) }
Hot sauce

Way to make it:

- ☐ Coarsely chop onion
- ☐ Spray 2-1/2-quart bowl with cooking spray
- ☐ Add onion, crumble in 1/2 pound ground beef, and sprinkle with 2 Tablespoons chili powder
- ☐ Stir with mixing spoon
- ☐ Microcook on HIGH for 5 minutes then stir to break up meat
- ☐ Coarsely chop 14-1/2-ounce can tomatoes, saving the juice
- ☐ Drain 16-ounce can kidney beans and 7-ounce can chopped green chilies
- ☐ Add the tomatoes, tomato juice, beans, and chilies to the meat mixture
- ☐ Microcook on HIGH, uncovered, for 20 minutes
- ☐ Add hot sauce to make it mean as you like

Apple of Your Black Eye

Makes one cup

(A tasty dish of peas that'll open your eyes)

Things you need:

Cutting board
Knife
1-quart bowl
1-cup measure
Teaspoon
Mixing spoon
Plastic wrap

Food you need:

1 scallion, chopped *(see page 55)*
1 cup canned and drained *(see page 66)* **or** frozen black-eyed peas
1/4 teaspoon garlic powder
1/8 teaspoon hot sauce
1/4 teaspoon seasoned salt
1/4 cup apple juice

Way to make it:

- ☐ Chop one scallion
- ☐ In a 1-quart bowl, mix the scallion, 1 cup of canned and drained **or** frozen black-eyed peas, 1/4 teaspoon garlic powder, 1/8 teaspoon hot sauce, 1/4 teaspoon seasoned salt, and 1/4 cup apple juice
- ☐ Cover with the plastic wrap and microcook on HIGH for 8 minutes

Steamed Spinach

Makes two servings

(So simple and sophisticated)

Things you need:

1-quart bowl
Plastic wrap

Food you need:

2 handfuls of fresh spinach
A splash of vinegar

Way to make it:

- ☐ Wash spinach well, but do **NOT** pat dry
- ☐ Place in a 1-quart bowl
- ☐ Cover with plastic wrap
- ☐ Microcook on HIGH for 1 minute 30 seconds
- ☐ Drain the excess liquid
- ☐ Splash with a dash of vinegar

Snappy Beans

Makes one serving

Things you need:

Strainer
Knife
Cutting board
Soup bowl
Plastic wrap

Food you need:

1/4 pound (4 ounces) fresh, frozen ***or*** (*ugh!*) canned green beans
2 Tablespoons water
Salt, pepper, and butter ***or*** margarine to taste

Way to make it:

- ☐ **If fresh,** wash 1/4 pound of green beans and drain in your strainer in the sink, then . . .
- ☐ . . . cut off the ends
- ☐ **If frozen,** open an 8-ounce package, take out half, and proceed as for fresh
- ☐ **If canned,** open the can, drain the beans, and dump out a 1/2 cup
- ☐ Pack beans tightly in a soup bowl
- ☐ Cover with plastic wrap and microcook on HIGH for . . .
- ☐ 3 minutes if fresh or frozen, 1 minute if canned
- ☐ Lightly sprinkle with salt and pepper
- ☐ Add a bit of butter ***or*** margarine if you wish

Spanish Rice

Makes two servings

Things you need:

Knife
Cutting board
2-1/2-quart bowl
Mixing spoon
Plastic wrap
1-cup measure

Food you need:

1 medium onion, coarsely chopped
1 green pepper, stemmed, seeded, and coarsely chopped } *(see page 55)*
3 fresh tomatoes (***or*** 1 cup canned tomatoes), chopped *(see page 56)*
Cooking spray
1 cup long-grain white rice *(see page 49)*
2 cups water
1/2 teaspoon salt
Optional: 1 canned green chile. You may also use hot pepper sauce to spice up this dish

Way to make it:

- ☐ Coarsely chop 1 onion, 1 green pepper, 3 fresh (***or*** 1 cup canned) tomatoes, and ***optional*** green chile pepper
- ☐ Place the vegetables in your 2-1/2-quart bowl
- ☐ Spray vegetables with a little cooking spray and stir with your mixing spoon
- ☐ Cover with plastic wrap and microcook on HIGH for 5 minutes (or until vegetables wilt)
- ☐ To the vegetables, add 1 cup rice, 2 cups water, and salt
- ☐ Stir together and cover bowl with plastic wrap
- ☐ Microcook on HIGH for 15 minutes
- ☐ Remove cover and stir. (***Optional:*** Add the hot sauce to your taste if you didn't add chile pepper)
- ☐ Microcook on HIGH for 12 minutes (or until rice is cooked and mixture is moist but not soupy)
- ☐ Eat right away

Stuffed Peppers

Makes one serving

Things you need:

Cutting board
Knife
Tablespoon
Pie plate
Mixing spoon
Wax paper
Paper towel

Food you need:

1 green pepper
Leftover Spanish rice *(see page 183)* ***OR:***
- 2 to 3 ounces (about 1/4 pound) of ground beef (**or** cubes of chicken)
- 2 Tablespoons finely chopped onions
- 2 Tablespoons chopped carrots } *(see pages 54 & 55)*
- 1/8 teaspoon garlic powder
- 1/2 cup cooked brown **or** white rice *(see page 49)*
- 2 canned tomatoes, either pre-chopped **or** chopped *(see page 56)*
- 1/2 cup tomato juice (from the canned tomatoes **or** canned tomato juice **or**, *in a real pinch*, 1/3 cup ketchup diluted in 1/2 cup water)

Way to make it:

- ☐ Cut top off pepper, remove insides, and trim the bottom so that the pepper will stand up, making sure you don't cut the whole bottom off or you'll have the rice falling out of the huge hole onto your shoes
- ☐ With Tablespoon, stuff pepper with leftover Spanish rice dish

OR . . .

- ☐ Chop pepper top and put into pie plate
- ☐ Crumble beef into pie plate
- ☐ Chop onions, carrots, and tomato

- ☐ Add 1/8 teaspoon garlic powder
- ☐ Add to pie plate and stir around with your mixing spoon
- ☐ Cover (with a plate ***or*** wax paper)
- ☐ Microcook on HIGH for 2 to 3 minutes (meat should no longer be pink)
- ☐ Pat fat off meat with paper towel
- ☐ Stir in the rice and half of the tomato juice
- ☐ Spoon the mixture into the shell of the pepper
- ☐ Pour a little of the tomato sauce (***or*** juice) on the pie plate
- ☐ Position green pepper in the middle of the plate
- ☐ Microcook on HIGH for 10 minutes (the pepper should be wilted when done)
- ☐ Let stand for 3 to 4 minutes to cool down before eating

White Sauce

Makes one cup

Things you need:

1-cup measure
Tablespoon

Food you need:

1 Tablespoon butter ***or*** margarine
2 Tablespoons cornstarch
1 cup chicken stock

Way to make it:

- ☐ Put 1 Tablespoon of butter ***or*** margarine in your 1-cup measure
- ☐ Microcook on HIGH for 30 seconds
- ☐ With your Tablespoon, stir in 2 Tablespoons of cornstarch
- ☐ Microcook the mixture on HIGH for 15 seconds
- ☐ Add 1 cup chicken stock, 1/4 cup at a time, stirring around with your Tablespoon ***and. . .***
- ☐ . . .after each addition, microcook on HIGH for 15 seconds
- ☐ Remove from the oven, let rest 5 minutes before using, then stir again

HINT: Use white sauce to endow everyday meats and vegetables with regal splendor. A quick and easy way to make people think you harbor secret and deep culinary talents.

Candlelight Chicken

Makes 2 servings

Things you need:

Glass pie plate
Strainer
1-cup measure
Tablespoon

Food you need:

Cooking spray
2 pre-cooked chicken breasts *(see page 71)*, each sliced into 4 pieces
1/2 box frozen whole leaf spinach, defrosted and drained
1 cup white sauce *(it's over there ☞)*
1/4 cup Parmesan cheese
Seasoned salt

Way to make it:

- ☐ Spray your glass pie plate lightly with cooking spray
- ☐ Squeeze all the water out of a defrosted 1/2 box of frozen whole leaf spinach
- ☐ Spread the spinach evenly over the pie plate
- ☐ With your Tablespoon, spoon 1/2 cup of the white sauce over the spinach
- ☐ Place the 2 pre-cooked and sliced chicken breasts over the spinach mixture
- ☐ Mix the remaining 1/2 cup of white sauce with 1/4 cup Parmesan cheese
- ☐ Spoon the white sauce and cheese mixture over the chicken
- ☐ Sprinkle lightly with the seasoned salt
- ☐ Microcook, uncovered, on HIGH for 2 minutes

Oven cleaning secret

This helps loosen grease and soil. It's cheap, easy, chemical-free, and makes the whole place smell good.

Things you need:

1-quart measure
2 cups water
1 whole lemon ***or*** 1 Tablespoon bottled lemon juice

Way to make it:

- Put 2 cups of water in your 1-quart measure
- Cut the lemon into four wedges and add to the water (no need to squeeze or anything) ***or*** add 1 Tablespoon bottled lemon juice
- Place the 1-quart measure in your microwave and cook on HIGH for 10 minutes
- Now just wipe down the oven with a clean, soft cloth!

Time to Clean the Oven Pasta Sauce

Makes one quart
(enough to dress one pound
of pasta and the inside of your microwave)

Things you need:

Cutting board
Knife
2-1/2-quart bowl
Can opener
Teaspoon
Plastic wrap

Food you need:

1 small onion, chopped *(see page 55)*
1/2 pound chopped beef
1 teaspoon garlic powder
One 28-ounce can of crushed tomatoes in purée
1 teaspoon Italian seasoning
1/2 teaspoon each of salt and pepper
1 teaspoon sugar
Optional: One 4-ounce can of mushroom stems and pieces
Parmesan cheese
Cooked pasta *(see page 47)*

Way to make it:

- ☐ Chop a small onion
- ☐ Crumble the meat into a 2-1/2-quart bowl
- ☐ Add the small chopped onion and 1 teaspoon garlic powder
- ☐ Stir with your mixing spoon; microcook on HIGH for 5 minutes
- ☐ Remove from oven, and add the tomatoes and purée
- ☐ Add 1 teaspoon Italian seasoning, 1/2 teaspoon salt, 1/2 teaspoon pepper, and 1 teaspoon sugar and stir with the mixing spoon
- ☐ Cover with plastic wrap, return to oven, and cook on HIGH for 20 minutes. ***OR,*** if you want to add the ***optional*** mushrooms ...
- ☐ ... stir and add the 4-ounce can of mushrooms after 15 minutes of cooking and microcook on HIGH for an additional 5 minutes
- ☐ Let stand 10 minutes before serving
- ☐ Serve over hot pasta and sprinkle with Parmesan cheese

TIP: May be kept covered and refrigerated up to one week, ***or*** frozen two months.

Micro Play Dough

Makes one heckofa good time
(just don't eat it)

Things you need:

1-quart glass measure
Mixing spoon
Paper towel
Plate

Food you need:

8-ounce box baking soda
1/2 cup cornstarch
1/2 cup cold water

Way to make it:

- ☐ In a 1-quart glass measure, combine 8 ounces of baking soda, 1/2 cup cornstarch, and 1/2 cup cold water
- ☐ Stir with your mixing spoon until well blended
- ☐ Microcook on HIGH for 4 minutes, stirring every minute
- ☐ Plop on a plate and cover with a damp paper towel
- ☐ Cool well, but *don't* refrigerate
- ☐ Knead gently and you're ready to play

Treats

How to peel and core an apple

Take your vegetable peeler and start stripping the apple from the top (the stem) down. Peel ribbons of skin all around the apple until it's naked.*

To core the apple, hold a sharp knife perpendicular to the top of the apple and cut around the stem in a circle. You can then remove the core.

For baked apples ☞☞☞

Peel the apple as above, only stop 1/4 of the way down. This leaves the natural skin to hold the apple together when it gets all mushy from cooking.

** Hmm, there's something about this recipe that a-peels to me. Get it, get it?—Ed.*
Too bad I'm not boiling a lobster. Get it, get it?—Auth.

Baked Apples

Makes two servings

Things you need:

Cutting board
Knife
Vegetable peeler
Teaspoon
Glass pie plate
Paper towel

Food you need:

2 medium apples, washed and cored *(see page on your left ☜)*
1 teaspoon raisins per apple
1/2 teaspoon cinnamon per apple
1 teaspoon sugar ***or*** artificial sweetener per apple
1/2 cup apple juice

Way to make it:

- ☐ Wash apple and remove core with a sharp knife, but . . .
  DON'T CUT ALL THE WAY THROUGH TO THE BOTTOM
- ☐ With a vegetable peeler, peel skin from top 1/4 of apple
- ☐ Fill center of apple (where the core was) with 1 teaspoon of raisins per apple
- ☐ Sprinkle 1/2 teaspoon cinnamon and 1 teaspoon sweetener over the top of the apples
- ☐ Place the apples on your pie plate and fill the center cores with apple juice
- ☐ Cover with paper towel and microcook on HIGH for 6 minutes
- ☐ Let stand 5 minutes covered

Apple Crisp

Makes four servings

Things you need:

Vegetable peeler	Mixing spoon	1-quart bowl
Cutting board	Glass pie plate	1-cup measure
Knife	Teaspoon	Tablespoon

Food you need:

2 apples, peeled *(see page 192)*
1 teaspoon lemon juice (fresh ***or*** bottled)
1/3 cup sugar
1/3 cup rolled oats (it's in the store — you'll find it, you'll find it)*
1/2 teaspoon cinnamon
2 Tablespoons butter ***or*** margarine

Way to make it:

- ☐ Peel apples with vegetable peeler
- ☐ Cut the peeled apple into slices, discarding the core
- ☐ Place the apple slices in your pie plate any old way and sprinkle with 1 teaspoon fresh ***or*** bottled lemon juice
- ☐ In a 1-quart bowl, add 1/3 cup of sugar, 1/3 cup rolled oats, and 1/2 teaspoon of cinnamon
- ☐ Add 2 Tablespoons butter ***or*** margarine, crumbled in small pieces, to the oat mixture; then mix lightly with your mixing spoon
- ☐ Sprinkle the oat mixture on top of the apples
- ☐ Microcook on HIGH for 10 minutes
- ☐ Cool before serving

** What the heck is THAT?—Ed.*

It's oatmeal, dummy.—Auth.

Why didn't you just say so?—Ed.

It's called being a specialist. You can charge more money if nobody knows what you're talking about.—Auth.

I NEVER know what you're talking about.—Ed.

YOU are a special case.—Auth.

College Coffee Cake

Makes one cake, 8 pieces

Things you need:

Any old cup
Fork
1-cup measure
9-inch glass pie plate
Tablespoon
Mixing spoon
Knife
Teaspoon

Food you need:

2 cups prepared biscuit mix (like Bisquick)
1 egg, beaten
2/3 cup water
2 Tablespoons sugar
2 Tablespoons butter ***or*** margarine
1/3 cup sugar
1 teaspoon cinnamon

Way to make it:

- ☐ Crack an egg into a cup
- ☐ Beat it with a fork for about 10 seconds (it will be a lemony-yellow when mixed)
- ☐ Place 2 cups prepared biscuit mix, the beaten egg, 2/3 cup water, and 2 Tablespoons sugar in a pie plate
- ☐ Stir with your mixing spoon until smooth (egg needs to be well distributed in batter)
- ☐ With your knife, cut 2 Tablespoons of butter ***or*** margarine into small pieces and drop on top of batter
- ☐ Sprinkle top with 2 Tablespoons of sugar
- ☐ Sprinkle with 1 teaspoon of cinnamon
- ☐ Microcook, uncovered, on HIGH for 10 minutes
- ☐ Let stand for 10 minutes
- ☐ Cut into wedges with your knife to serve

Easy Cheesecake

Makes one cake, 8 pieces

Things you need:

2-1/2-quart bowl
1-cup measure
Mixing spoon
Teaspoon

Food you need:

8 ounces ready-made whipped topping ("chemical" kind or the real aerosol stuff)
8 ounces (1 cup) **LIGHT** cream cheese, softened
1/3 cup sugar
1/2 cup sour cream
2 teaspoons vanilla
1 ready-made graham cracker pie crust

Way to make it:

- ☐ If you bought the frozen "whipped cream," take it out of the freezer
- ☐ Take 8 ounces LIGHT cream cheese out of the refrigerator and allow to warm 10 minutes
- ☐ Add cream cheese to 2-1/2-quart bowl along with 1/3 cup sugar
- ☐ Beat cheese/sugar mixture with your mixing spoon until well mixed
- ☐ Add 1/2 cup sour cream and 2 teaspoons vanilla and blend well again
- ☐ With the mixing spoon, beat in (mix like heck) the whipped cream, making sure all ingredients are now blended
- ☐ With the mixing spoon, spoon the mixture into the ready-made pie shell
- ☐ Cool 4 hours in fridge ***or*** if you go to the University of Wisconsin or live in Minneapolis/St. Paul, and it's January, put outside for about 3 seconds

End-of-Month Reeses*

Makes 24 candies

Things you need:

1-quart bowl
1-cup measure
Tablespoon
Plastic wrap
Teaspoon
Wax paper
Pie plate

Food you need:

1/2 cup smooth peanut butter
6 ounces (1 small package) chocolate chips
1/2 cup dry-roasted, salted peanuts

Way to make it:

- ☐ In a 1-quart bowl, place 1/2 cup of smooth peanut butter and 6 ounces (a small package) of chocolate chips and mix with your Tablespoon
- ☐ Cover with plastic wrap and microcook on HIGH for 2 minutes, until melted
- ☐ Stir with your Tablespoon
- ☐ Add 1/2 cup of dry-roasted, salted peanuts and mix again
- ☐ Drop by teaspoons on wax paper placed on the pie plate
- ☐ Refrigerate until set — about 15 minutes

* *You DO mean "recess," don't you?—Ed.*

Oh, yes. I'm a VERY poor speller.—Auth.

Choco-Moose

Makes four servings

Things you need:

1-cup measure   Blender   4 custard cups

Food you need:

1/4 cup boiling water
6 ounces chocolate chips (that's 1 small bag for mankind)
1/4 cup sugar
1 egg
1/2 cup whole milk

Way to make it:

- ☐ Put 1/4 cup water in a 1-cup glass measuring cup
- ☐ Microcook on HIGH for 5 minutes
- ☐ While water is heating, put 6 ounces (1 small bag) chocolate chips in blender
- ☐ Whirl on HIGH until the chips are ground finely
- ☐ Remove the water from the microwave
- ☐ With blender running, add hot water to the chips and continue to run until chocolate is melted. USE THE HOLE IN THE TOP OF THE BLENDER THAT IS COVERED WITH A LITTLE GLASS CAP. JUST REMOVE THIS CAP — DO NOT REMOVE ENTIRE TOP FOR THIS PROCESS
- ☐ Add 1/4 cup sugar and 1 egg to blender*
- ☐ Turn blender on HIGH speed to mix
- ☐ With the blender running, pour in 1/2 cup milk
- ☐ Blend for one minute
- ☐ Pour mixture into dessert cups (***or*** any 4-ounce containers) and chill well for 3 hours

** Hey, what about Rocky Balboa?—Ed.*

What? A new boyfriend?—Auth.

No, no. The raw egg. You can't eat raw eggs.—Ed.

Oh, the egg. It "cooks" in the hot water.—Auth.

Krispy Kritters

Makes 12 cookies

Things you need:

Glass pie plate
Tablespoon
1-quart bowl
1-cup measure
Mixing spoon

Food you need:

Cooking spray
2 Tablespoons butter ***or*** margarine
A package of miniature marshmallows
3 cups crispy rice cereal

Way to make it:

- ☐ Spray pie plate with cooking spray
- ☐ Place 2 Tablespoons butter ***or*** margarine in your 1-quart bowl
- ☐ Microcook on HIGH for 15 seconds until melted
- ☐ With your mixing spoon, stir in 3 cups of marshmallows
- ☐ Microcook on HIGH for 1 minute to soften
- ☐ Stir mixture with your mixing spoon, then microcook on HIGH for 1 minute more
- ☐ Stir mixture until smooth
- ☐ Add 3 cups crispy rice cereal and mix well
- ☐ Press cereal mixture into pie plate
- ☐ Cool and cut into serving pieces

Party Animals & Vegetables

Oh no! I've got that Saturday Night Fever again!*

Even in small spaces, we all like to entertain occasionally. Here are a few tips to maximize your fun and minimize the work.

- **Prepare all the dips and sauces the day before the party.** This allows the flavors to blend and frees you up to do your nails or watch the game or maybe even clean the house a little.†

- **Store the dips in the containers in which they will be served,** covered tightly with plastic wrap and refrigerated.

- **Invest in an inexpensive Styrofoam cooler.** This makes an excellent airtight dry food storage box most of the time. Just unload the food and fill with ice when you're ready to party.

- **Whip up a batch of Slushes** in your blender using concentrated lemonade mix. Whirl in a banana or a few washed strawberries for a tropical treat. Frozen drink mixes are expensive *(there are some more ideas over there☞)* .

- **Mix juices — such as orange, cranberry, or grapefruit — with club soda** (2/3 juice to 1/3 club soda) for a festive drink that stretches the more expensive juices.

- **Buy frozen cooked and peeled shrimp** in supermarkets or food warehouses. All you need to do is defrost by placing them in a strainer and running under cold water for a few minutes. Because you are not paying for the weight of the shells, often these are cheaper than "fresh" shrimp. ***HINT:*** Most shrimp are previously frozen, unless you catch them yourself.

* *You're showing your age, dearie.—Ed.*

At least *I'm* not running around with high school juniors!—Auth.

That's how much you know. Dennis is a senior!*—Ed.*

I hear the wedding bells now!—Auth

† *Nah!—Ed.*

- **Substitute veggies for crackers and chips when serving dips.** Celery and carrots are great. So are slices of yellow squash, scallions, and broccoli florets. There are more suggestions on the next page. They are less expensive, don't create crumbs to clean up, and are better for you.

- **Wash veggies well before serving** (I knew you'd remember). They then can be cut and stored tightly wrapped in plastic and refrigerated for several days.

- **Serve the food and drinks with colorful cocktail napkins instead of plates.** They don't cost as much, your guests eat less, and there's no clean up!

Some More Slushes

Things you need:

Blender

Food you need:

One 8-ounce can frozen lemonade
1/2 cup cranberry juice
1 cup ice

Way to make it:

- [ ] Place everything in your blender and whirl on HIGH until frothy

Variations:
Instead of the lemonade and cranberry juice try:

- One 8-ounce can frozen orange juice and 1/2 cup strawberries

OR

- One 8-ounce can frozen white grape juice and 1/2 cup frozen melon balls

Party vegetable ideas

(See dips on pages 206 to 208; also see below to cut this stuff up nicely)

Broccoli
Buy a whole head of broccoli, wash it, and whack off the heavy stem. Save the stem and use for broccoli slaw *(see recipe, page 213)*. With a small knife, trim and separate the florets into dipping-size pieces.

Carrots
Peel the carrots, put on a cutting board and cut in half lengthwise. Place flat side down and cut in half lengthwise again. This will give you four pieces. Line them up on your board and cut across them in about 2-inch pieces to create nice even carrot spears.

HINT: Pre-packaged "baby" carrots are available in many markets. They don't need to be peeled and are already in bite-sized pieces. Although they are more expensive, they are a real timesaver for both party platters and daily cooking.

Cauliflower
Rinse well, cut off the stem end and discard. With a sharp paring knife *(see page 18)*, cut into serving pieces, just like with broccoli *(see page 213)*. Make sure you cut the stems close to the flower. They shouldn't look like miniature shade trees.

Celery
On your cutting board, cut off discolored ends with a sharp knife. Wash well, as celery tends to be gritty. Cut each stalk into 2-inch pieces.

Cherry tomatoes
Just wash and remove the green stems on top. Nature has already made them finger-food-size for you.

Mushrooms
Trim off stem ends, wipe with wet paper towels to remove dirt. Do not soak. Serve whole.

Olives
Just drain out of the can or jar *(see page 66)* and sprinkle green and black ones around the platter.

Peppers
Wash, seed, and remove the membrane from bell pepper *(see page 55)*. Slice into 1-inch strips. Even though yellow and red peppers cost a bit more, buy one or two to mix with the green pepper strips to liven up the color on your party platter.

Scallions
Trim off root end and cut tops to manageable size, about 3 inches. You can save the tops, chop them finely and add to sour cream for onion dip.

Squash
Yellow squash and zucchini both make great fat free "chips." Just wash them well and cut into rounds. Combine both colors to make a more festive presentation.

Fiesta Dip

Makes 2-1/2 cups

Things you need:

Can opener
Cutting board
Knife
2-1/2-quart bowl
1-cup measure
Mixing spoon
Paper towel

Food you need:

One 7-ounce can of chopped green chilies, drained *(see page 66)*
One 16-ounce can refried beans
1 can cheddar cheese soup (undiluted)
1/2 cup salsa

Way to make it:

- ☐ Open and drain a 7-ounce can of green chilies and chop on your cutting board
- ☐ Add chilies, 16-ounce can refried beans, and 1 can of undiluted cheddar cheese soup in your 2-1/2-quart mixing bowl
- ☐ Stir with your mixing spoon to blend
- ☐ Cover bowl with a paper towel and microcook on HIGH for 3 minutes
- ☐ Add 1/2 cup of salsa, stir well, cover again, then microcook on HIGH for 3 minutes more
- ☐ Stir and serve

Spinach Dip

Makes 4 cups

Things you need:

Strainer
Mixing spoon
2-1/2-quart bowl
1-cup measure
Plastic wrap

Food you need:

1 package frozen chopped spinach, defrosted and drained
1 package dry vegetable soup mix*
One 16-ounce container of sour cream
1/2 cup mayonnaise
Crackers and/or cut up vegetables *(see page 204)*

Way to make it:

- ☐ Defrost one package of frozen chopped spinach
- ☐ Drain well in a strainer, squeezing out all liquid
- ☐ Mix 1 package vegetable soup mix with one 16-ounce container of sour cream in a 2-1/2-quart bowl
- ☐ Mix in 1/2 cup mayonnaise and the spinach
- ☐ Cover with plastic wrap and refrigerate at least 2 hours
- ☐ Stir well before serving with assorted crackers and/or cut vegetables

*** I like Knorr Spring Vegetable—Auth.**

Dill Dip

Makes 1/2 cup*

Things you need:

1-cup measure
Soup bowl
Teaspoon
Fork

Food you need:

1/2 cup sour cream ***or*** 1/2 cup plain yogurt
1/2 teaspoon dried dill
Raw vegetables *(see pages 204 & 205)* and/or crackers

Way to make it:

- ☐ Put 1/2 cup sour cream ***or*** 1/2 cup yogurt in a soup bowl
- ☐ Add 1/2 teaspoon dried dill
- ☐ Blend well with a fork
- ☐ Serve with raw vegetables and/or crackers

** Enough for one teensy, weensy party!—Ed.*

Yeah. One of yours. But anybody else can double the recipe or more.—Auth.

Bacon Wraps

Makes about 10 pieces

Things you need:

Can opener
1-quart bowl
1-cup measure
Mixing spoon
Cutting board
Knife
Toothpicks
Paper towel
Glass pie plate

Food you need:

1 can whole water chestnuts, drained *(see page 66)*
1/8 cup soy sauce
4 slices of bacon *(see page 62)*

Way to make it:

- ☐ Drain 1 can water chestnuts
- ☐ Add 1/8 cup soy sauce and water chestnuts in your 1-quart bowl
- ☐ Toss with your mixing spoon to coat
- ☐ Allow to marinate at least 15 minutes; **MEANWHILE . . .**
- ☐ Get your cutting board and knife and cut each piece of bacon into thirds
- ☐ Drain chestnuts and discard soy sauce
- ☐ Wrap each chestnut in 1/3 piece of bacon, secure with toothpick
- ☐ Put 2 sheets of paper towel on pie plate
- ☐ Arrange chestnuts like spokes of a wheel on top of towel
- ☐ Microcook on HIGH for 7 minutes ***or*** until bacon is crisp*

** Walter says the bacon never gets crisp.—Ed.*

Who's Walter, or shouldn't I ask?—Auth.

Walter's your illustrator, you hockey puck!—Ed.

Oh! That Walter! He can't get his bacon crisp? Sounds like you two should get together.—Auth.

You know, that's not a bad idea. Maybe I can, uh, teach him how to crisp his bacon.—Ed.

Uh, is this book almost finished?—Auth.

Party Dogs*

Makes 96 pieces

Things you need:

Cutting board
Knife
1-cup measure
2-1/2-quart bowl
Mixing spoon
Plastic wrap
Toothpicks

Food you need:

2 pounds of hot dogs
3/4 cup mustard (Dijon works best, but whatever)
1 cup grape jelly (yes, you read right)

Way to make it:

- ☐ Cut each hot dog into six pieces
- ☐ Place 3/4 cup mustard and 1 cup grape jelly in a 2-1/2-quart bowl
- ☐ Stir with your mixing spoon to blend
- ☐ Add hot dogs to bowl
- ☐ Cover with plastic wrap
- ☐ Microcook on HIGH for 5 minutes
- ☐ Stir and serve immediately with toothpicks

* *"Geez, this looks awful,"* said the Editor, who inadvertently walked into the test kitchen for some free food.

"Just taste it," said the Author before she tried it herself, just in case.

"Hmmm, yummy," said the Editor.

And you will love it, too.—Auth.

I gotta give some to Walter.—Ed.

Party Caviar

Makes about 2 cups

Things you need:

Cutting board
Knife
Paper towel
Microsafe plate
Tablespoon
2-1/2-quart bowl
Teaspoon

Food you need:

1 ripe tomato
1 medium eggplant, cut as described below
1 Tablespoon finely chopped onion *(see page 55)*
1 Tablespoon chopped scallion *(see page 56)*
1/2 teaspoon garlic powder
2 Tablespoons lemon juice (fresh ***or*** bottled)
1 Tablespoon olive oil
Salt and pepper to taste

Way to make it:

- ☐ Pierce the tomato in several places with your knife
- ☐ Place the tomato on the paper towel in the microwave and microcook on HIGH for 1 minute
- ☐ Remove from the microwave and set aside
- ☐ Place the eggplant on a microsafe plate and cut a 4-inch to 6-inch slit, 1-inch deep, lengthwise
- ☐ Microcook on HIGH for 10 minutes (it is done when soft and collapsed*)
- ☐ Remove from the microwave and let stand 2 minutes, then use the Tablespoon to scoop the pulp from the skin and put on the cutting board

(continued)

** Just like me!—Ed.*

Nobody's interested.—Auth.

THE RECIPES

- ☐ Cut the eggplant meat into bite-size chunks and place in the 2-1/2-quart bowl
- ☐ With your Tablespoon, stir in 1 Tablespoon chopped onion, 1 Tablespoon chopped scallion, and 1/2 teaspoon garlic powder
- ☐ Cut the microwaved tomato in half and squeeze out the water and the seeds
- ☐ Chop the tomato finely and add to the eggplant
- ☐ Add lemon juice, olive oil, and salt and pepper to taste and stir with the Tablespoon
- ☐ Let the "caviar" cool and serve with hard bread, toast, and/or crackers

Broccoli Slaw

Makes about 2 cups

Things you need:

Cutting board
Knife
Grater
1-quart bowl
Tablespoon

Food you need:

1 broccoli stem, grated } *(like on page 52)*
1 carrot, grated }
1/2 small onion
Bottled coleslaw dressing

Way to make it:

- ☐ Wash the vegetables — no need to peel the carrot unless it's gross
- ☐ Cut the stem off of the broccoli, reserving the florets for another use*
- ☐ Cut the stem end off a carrot
- ☐ Peel the onion and slice thinly
- ☐ Coarsely grate the carrot and broccoli stem with your grater
- ☐ Toss the veggies into a 1-quart bowl
- ☐ Add 4 Tablespoons (more or less to your taste) prepared coleslaw dressing and toss well

HINT: This tastes better if allowed to cool in the fridge for about 3 hours before serving.

** What's a floret, and what can I use it for?—Ed.*

Florets is the chef word for the part of the broccoli you eat. Use it as a healthy snack.—Auth.

Or as a bouquet at the prom.—Ed.

What planet did you say you were from?—Auth.

How the shell do I devein a shrimp?

Peel it first. Grab the shrimp by the tail. Start peeling at the large end; the shell will come off in a spiral. You may leave the tail on if you wish. I think it's prettier, but you will have to take it off before eating.* It is easier to shell and devein raw shrimp than cooked.

There will be a black vein that runs down the back of the shrimp. Take a sharp paring knife and make a small cut along the back of the shrimp. This will release the vein and allow you to rinse it away under cold running water.

1 Holding the shrimp by the tail, start peeling from the large end.

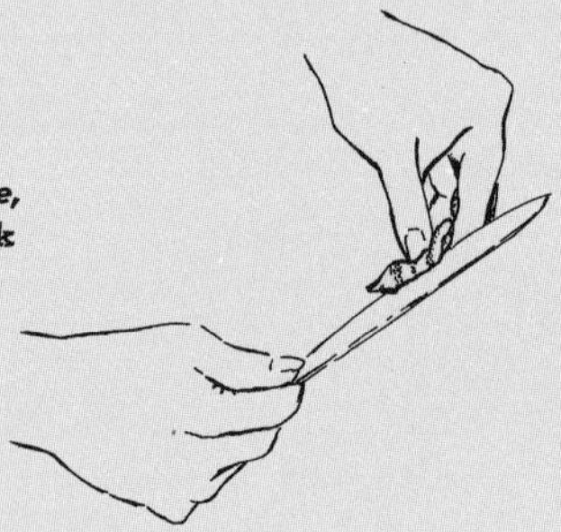

2 With a sharp paring knife, make a cut along the back of the shrimp.

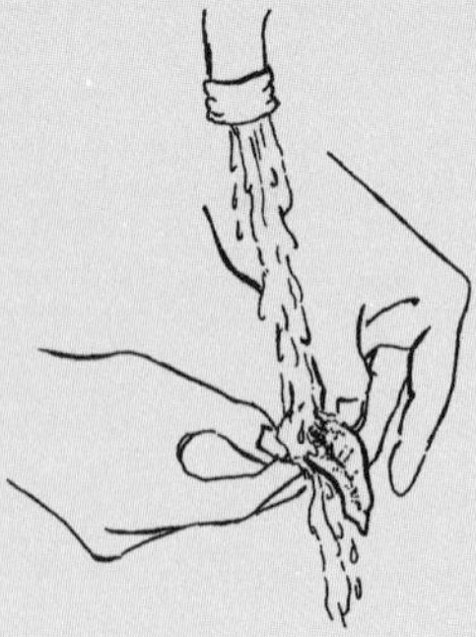

3 Run the shrimp under cold water.

** It's a pain.—Ed.*

Icy Shrimp

Makes 24 shrimp

Things you need:

Pie Plate | Cutting board | Knife

Food you need:

24 large shrimp, peeled and deveined *(see page over there ☜)*
Lemon juice (fresh ***or*** 1 teaspoon bottled)
Barbecue sauce ***or*** cocktail sauce *(bottled* ***or*** *use recipe below)*

Way to make it:

- ☐ Place shrimp on single layer around edge of plate, with tails facing into the center *(help is on the left page ☜)*
- ☐ With your knife, cut the lemon in half, then squeeze the juice onto the shrimp —WATCH FOR THE SEEDS (***or*** use 1 teaspoon bottled lemon juice)
- ☐ Microcook on HIGH for 2 to 3 minutes
- ☐ Cover and let stand 1 to 2 minutes to finish cooking
- ☐ Cool before serving by immediately refrigerating
- ☐ Dip in barbecue sauce ***or*** cocktail sauce

Cocktail Sauce

Things you need:

1-quart bowl | Tablespoon | 1-cup measure | Teaspoon

Food you need:

1/2 cup ketchup
1 teaspoon horseradish (red ***or*** white)
1 teaspoon fresh ***or*** bottled lemon juice

Way to make it:

- ☐ In your 1-quart bowl, use a Tablespoon to mix 1/2 cup ketchup with 1 teaspoon horseradish and 1 teaspoon lemon juice
- ☐ Mix well and serve

Don't forget fruit as a party food. It's good for you all the time, but adds color and a bit of sweet to counterbalance the saltiness usually found in party fare. Especially nice in the summer months, fruits are easy to prepare in advance and any leftovers become an easy, quick breakfast the next day — alone or with cottage cheese, sour cream, or over cereal.

Make sure you wash all fruit well before serving.

Apples Don't bother to peel, just cut into wedges. Use both green and red varieties. ***Warning!*** Cut apples must be stored in water with lemon juice added or they will turn brown rapidly.

Grapes Use red and green — make sure they are seedless.

Melon Both cantaloupe and honeydew sliced in small wedges or peeled and cut into chunks. Don't use canned.

Pears Both brown and green — don't peel.

Pineapple Cut in chunks or spears. Fresh is best, but a pain to cut up. Use canned in a pinch.

Strawberries Leave the stem on to create a little holder.

TIP: As the food-loving Europeans have known for hundreds of years, fruit goes *great* with cheese. Add some grapes or apples to your cheese platters, too!

Well, that about wraps things up.—Auth.
Wraps — reminds me of Walter—Ed.
What?—Auth.
Wraps. Bacon Wraps. That's what brought me and Walter together.—Ed.
Walter and I.—Auth.
Oh! So you're going with Walter, too?—Ed.
Say goodbye to the nice folks.—Auth.
Goodbye to the nice folks.—Ed.

The Index

WORD SEEK

The Kitchenless™ Cookbook makes a great gift...

...for college students, singles or couples, boaters and RV campers, seniors — *anybody* who has to fit good eating into an impossible schedule or surroundings.

A shoebox of staples, a preprinted shopping list, and less than 20 minutes, and they're ready for a meal, a nutritious snack, or even a party!

Just send the card below to:

InterMedia Publishing, Inc.
P.O. Box 291506
Davie, FL 33329-1506

YES, please send The Kitchenless™ Cookbook to the address below! Enclosed is a check or money order for $_________. (Books are sent *priority mail*. $21.95 per copy, plus $3.95 postage and handling for the first book, $1.95 for each additional copy to the same address. Payable in U.S. funds. Florida residents, please add 6% sales tax to help pay for I-95 or whatever.)

Name ____

Street address ______________________________________

City _______________ State _________ Zip Code _______________

Gift card to read: ___________________________________

____

The Kitchenless™ Cookbook makes a great gift...

...for college students, singles or couples, boaters and RV campers, seniors — anybody who has to fit good eating into an impossible schedule or surroundings.

A shoebox of staples, a preprinted shopping list, and less than 20 minutes, and they're ready for a meal, a nutritious snack, or even a party!

Just send the card below to:

InterMedia Publishing, Inc.
P.O. Box 291506
Davie, FL 33329-1506

YES, please send The Kitchenless™ Cookbook to the address below! Enclosed is a check or money order for $_________. (Books are sent priority mail. $21.95 per copy, plus $2.95 postage and handling for the first book, $.95 for each additional copy to the same address. Payable in U.S. funds. Florida residents, please add 6% sales tax to help pay for I-95 or whatever.)

Name ____

Street address ____________________________________

City __________ State _________ Zip Code ____________

Gift card to read: _________________________________

____

The Kitchenless™ Cookbook makes a great gift...

...for college students, singles or couples, boaters and RV campers, seniors — anybody who has to fit good eating into an impossible schedule or surroundings.

A shoebox of staples, a preprinted shopping list, and less than 20 minutes, and they're ready for a meal, a nutritious snack, or even a party!

Just send the card below to:

InterMedia Publishing, Inc.
P.O. Box 291506
Davie, FL 33329-1506

YES, please send The Kitchenless™ Cookbook to the address below! Enclosed is a check or money order for $__________. (Books are sent priority mail. $21.95 per copy, plus $2.95 postage and handling for the first book, $.95 for each additional copy to the same address. Payable in U.S. funds. Florida residents, please add 6% sales tax to help pay for I-95 or whatever.)

Name ____

Street address____________________________________

City_____________ State ________ Zip Code _____________

Gift card to read:____________________________________

____